Eureka!

Eureka!

VOLUME 6: Sp-Z

Edited by
Linda Schmittroth,
Mary Reilly McCall
& Bridget Travers

AN IMPRINT OF GALE RESEARCH INC.,
AN INTERNATIONAL THOMPSON PUBLISHING COMPANY

I(T)P
Changing the Way the World Learns

NEW YORK • LONDON • BONN • BOSTON • DETROIT • MADRID
MELBOURNE • MEXICO CITY • PARIS • SINGAPORE • TOKYO
TORONTO • WASHINGTON • ALBANY NY • BELMONT CA • CINCINNATI OH

Eureka!

Scientific Discoveries and Inventions That Shaped the World

Edited by **Linda Schmittroth, Mary Reilly McCall, and Bridget Travers**

Staff

Carol DeKane Nagel, *Developmental Editor*
Jane Hoehner, *Contributing Editor*
Julie L. Carnagie, *Assistant Editor*
Thomas L. Romig, *U·X·L Publisher*

Shanna P. Heilveil, *Production Associate*
Evi Seoud, *Assistant Production Manager*
Mary Beth Trimper, *Production Director*

Margaret A. Chamberlain, *Permissions Associate (Pictures)*

Pamela A. E. Galbreath, *Cover and Page Designer*
Cynthia Baldwin, *Art Director*

∞™ This book is printed on acid-free paper that meets the minimum requirements of American National Standard for Information Sciences—Permanence Paper for Printed Library Materials, ANSI Z39.48-1984.

ISBN: 0-8103-9802-8 (Set)
ISBN: 0-8103-9803-6 (Volume 1)
ISBN: 0-8103-9804-4 (Volume 2)
ISBN: 0-8103-9805-2 (Volume 3)
ISBN: 0-8103-9806-0 (Volume 4)
ISBN: 0-8103-9807-9 (Volume 5)
ISBN: 0-8103-9808-7 (Volume 6)

Printed in the United States of America

I(T)P™

U·X·L is an imprint of Gale Research,
an International Thomson Publishing Company.

ITP logo is a trademark under license.

Table of Contents

Reader's Guide

Eureka! Scientific Discoveries and Inventions That Shaped the World features 600 entries on scientific inventions and discoveries that have made a great impact on the world—from the principle of buoyancy to the atomic bomb, from blood transfusion to microcomputers—and the people responsible for them. Written in nontechnical language, *Eureka!* explores such important inventions as the ancient craft of brick-making, but focuses primarily on significant breakthroughs from the Industrial Revolution to the present day, including the invention of the steam engine and the discoveries made possible by the Hubble Space Telescope.

Each *Eureka!* entry, whether on a well-known discovery or a lesser-known invention, identifies the person behind the breakthrough, the knowledge and technology that led to it, and how these advances changed the world in which we live.

Scope and Format

Eureka!'s 600 entries are arranged alphabetically over six volumes. Entries range from one-quarter to eight pages and often include sidebar boxes discussing important breakthroughs, such as firsts in space flight, and lesser-known facts, such as how a frog helped invent the electric battery. Boldfaced terms in the text direct the reader to related entries in the set, while cross-references at the ends of entries alert the reader to related entries not specifically mentioned in that entry. More than 430 photographs and original illustrations enliven and help explain the text.

Each *Eureka!* volume begins with a listing of the featured discoveries and inventions arranged by 37 scientific categories. This handy category listing lets users quickly identify and locate related discoveries and inventions. The comprehensive general index found at the end of each volume provides easy access to the people, theories, and discoveries and inventions mentioned throughout *Eureka!*

Special Thanks and Dedication

The editors dedicate this work to their husbands and to their daughters, Margie and Sara, along with all the children of St. Agatha School in Redford, Michigan, and Bingham Farms Elementary School in Bingham Farms, Michigan. They would also like to express their sincere appreciation to teacher Marlene Heitmanis and tutor and counselor Theresa McCall for their guidance on school curricula.

Comments and Suggestions

We welcome your comments on this work as well as your suggestions for topics to be featured in future editions of *Eureka! Scientific Discoveries and Inventions That Shaped the World.* Please write: Editors, *Eureka!* U·X·L, 835 Penobscot Bldg., Detroit, Michigan 48226-4094; call toll-free: 1-800-877-4253; or fax 1-313-877-6348.

Inventions and Discoveries by Subject

Bold numerals indicate volume numbers.

Civil engineering and construction

Clothing and textiles and their manufacture

Communications/ graphic arts

Computer science and mathematical devices

Electrical engineering/electricity

Electronics

Amplifier **1:** 54
Audiocassette **1:** 114
Calculator, pocket **2:** 228
Fax machine **3:** 449
LCD (liquid crystal display)
    4: 644
LED (light-emitting diode) **4:** 645
Magnetic recording **4:** 668
Microphone **4:** 697
Noise reduction system **4:** 744
Oscillator **4:** 765
Radio **5:** 874
Video recording **6:** 1130
Walkman **6:** 1141

Environmental sciences/ecology

Acid rain **1:** 9
Food chain **3:** 471
Gaia hypothesis **3:** 481
Greenhouse effect **3:** 513
Methane **4:** 694
Natural gas **4:** 723
Ozone **4:** 770
Radon **5:** 882
Recycling **5:** 884
Red tide **5:** 887

Everyday items

Aerosol spray **1:** 19
Baby bottle **1:** 127
Baby carrier/pouch **1:** 127
Bar code **1:** 135
Bath and shower **1:** 140
Calculator, pocket **2:** 228
Can opener **2:** 237
Car wash, automatic **2:** 252
Cash register **2:** 253
Chewing gum **2:** 264
Diaper, disposable **2:** 344
Dog biscuit **2:** 356
Electric blanket **2:** 381
Eraser **2:** 400
Fan **3:** 445
Fire extinguisher **3:** 462
Firefighting equipment **3:** 462

Flashlight **3:** 467
Instant coffee **3:** 580
Laundromat **4:** 642
Pen **5:** 814
Polystyrene **5:** 854
Post-it note **5:** 856
Stapler **6:** 1009
Swiss army knife **6:** 1038
Teaching aid **6:** 1045
Telephone answering device **6:** 1048
Toilet **6:** 1072
Toothbrush and toothpaste **6:** 1074
Traffic signal **6:** 1079
Tupperware **6:** 1100
Typing correction fluid **6:** 1104
Umbrella **6:** 1114
Vacuum bottle **6:** 1123
Waterbed **6:** 1143

Food/food science

Artificial sweetener **1:** 93
Baby food, commercial **1:** 128
Bread and crackers **1:** 180
Breakfast cereal **1:** 182
Can and canned food **2:** 234
Can opener **2:** 237
Chewing gum **2:** 264
Chocolate **2:** 266
Concentrated fruit juice **2:** 317
Doughnut **2:** 356
Fat substitute **3:** 448
Food preservation **3:** 472
Soda pop **5:** 938
Yogurt **6:** 1173

Geology

Continental drift **2:** 319
Cretaceous catastrophe **2:** 326
Earthquake **2:** 363
Earthquake measurement scale
    2: 365
Earth's core **2:** 368
Earth's mantle **2:** 371
Earth survey satellite **2:** 372
Mohorovicic discontinuity **4:** 705
Plate tectonics **5:** 843
Seismology **5:** 916
Uniformitarianism **6:** 1116

Metallurgy

Meteorology

Musical instruments

Navigation

Oceanography

Optics

Personal care items

Pharmacology

Physics

Security systems and related items

Sports, games, toys, and fads

Timepieces, measuring devices, and related items

Transportation

Weapons and related items

Picture Credits

The photographs appearing in *Eureka! Scientific Discoveries and Inventions That Shaped the World* were received from the following sources:

Eureka!

⋆⋆ Spacecraft, manned

After World War II (1939-45), scientists around the world were free to turn their attention from war to the exploration of outer space. The United States and the Soviet Union (now Russia), who had fought on the same side during that war, emerged from it only to spend the next half century engaged in a cold war with each other. A cold war is a state of rivalry that stops short of actual, full-scale war. Part of that rivalry showed itself in the race for dominance in space.

The Space Race

American Efforts

In 1961 newly elected president John F. Kennedy announced America's goal of landing on the Moon within eight years. In preparation for that historic achievement, Alan Shepard ascended into suborbital flight on board *Freedom 7* on May 5, 1961, spending 15 minutes and 22 seconds in flight before descending to Earth. He remained in the spacecraft until it splashed down in the Atlantic and a navy ship met him.

Virgil "Gus" Grissom went on another such flight in July 1961. John Glenn became the first American to orbit Earth on February 20, 1962, circling the planet three times in less than five hours. As a result of this accomplishment, Glenn became one of the most celebrated national heroes since Charles Lindbergh made the first solo transatlantic flight in 1927. The U.S. manned space program gained valuable public and media support.

President Dwight D. Eisenhower sponsored the creation of the National Aeronautics and Space Administration (NASA) because he wanted emerging space technology to be outside the control of the military.

Firsts in Manned Space Flight

April 12, 1961: Soviet Yuri Gagarin becomes the first person to fly in space, circling Earth in 108 minutes.

May 5, 1961: Alan Shepard becomes the first American to fly in space, spending 15 minutes, 22 seconds in flight.

February 20, 1962: John Glenn becomes the first American to orbit Earth, circling the planet three times in less than 5 hours.

June 16, 1963: Soviets send the first woman, Valentina Tereshkova, into orbit.

October 1964: Soviets launch the first three-person spacecraft.

March 18, 1965: Soviet cosmonaut Alexei Leonov takes the first space walk.

July 20, 1969: Americans Neil Armstrong and Edwin "Buzz" Aldrin become the first humans to walk on the Moon.

July 15, 1975: The *Apollo* and *Soyuz* take off on the first manned international cooperative space mission.

September 1980: A Cuban cosmonaut, Arnaldo Tomayo Mendez, becomes the first black person to fly in space, aboard Russia's *Soyuz 38.*

September 12, 1992: Mae C. Jemison becomes the first black woman in space, aboard the U.S. Space Shuttle *Endeavour.*

The orbits gave way to the *Gemini* program in 1964. Its goal was to design a two-man spacecraft and develop the skills and technology necessary for achieving a lunar landing.

The United States *Gemini* spacecraft consisted of two sections: a capsule capable of carrying two astronauts and an adapter section. Between March 1965 and November 1966, ten manned *Gemini* spacecraft were sent into orbit. Their missions were:

- to extend mission times,

- to practice and make perfect orbital maneuvering, rendezvous (pronounced ron-day-voo; to meet at a prearranged place), and docking techniques, and

• to train astronauts in extra-vehicular (outside the spacecraft) activity.

Highlights on *Gemini* flights included Ed White's 21-minute spacewalk, *Gemini 6* and *7*'s rendezvous in space, and *Gemini 10*'s docking with a rocket and firing its engine for a new orbit.

NASA applied the advances made during the *Gemini* missions to the *Apollo* spacecraft, the first manned vehicle to land on the Moon. The craft consisted of three parts: the command module where three astronauts would travel; the service module that carried fuel, oxygen, water, the electrical system, and communications equipment; and the lunar module, which would make the actual descent and lift-off from the Moon's surface.

The first *Apollo* missions were tests of the command and service modules and the ability of the command and lunar modules to rendezvous

Apollo 11's Moon landing has been described as the greatest achievement of the modern world.

and dock. Disaster struck in 1967. On a ground test of *Apollo 1*, three astronauts—Gus Grissom, Ed White, and Roger Chaffee—died after an electrical spark ignited the pure oxygen of their cabin, causing fire and toxic fumes to spread in seconds. As a result of this tragedy the program was delayed as questions arose concerning the spacecraft's safety. More than 1,500 modifications were made to the command module to ensure astronauts' safety.

The Moon Landing

The *Apollo* spacecraft was ready for flight in October 1968. After several "rehearsal" flights, *Apollo 11* was launched on July 16, 1969, with astronauts Neil Armstrong Michael Collins, and Edwin "Buzz" Aldrin on board. Four days later, Aldrin and Armstrong descended into the Moon's Sea of Tranquility in the lunar module *Eagle*. As Armstrong stepped down onto the Moon's surface, he uttered the now-famous words, "That's one

Apollo 15 astronaut David R. Scott studies a boulder on the slope of the Hadley Delta. The lunar rover is at right.

small step for man, one giant leap for mankind." *Apollo 11* has been described as the greatest achievement of the modern world.

America next turned its attention to space stations. Its first space station, *Skylab,* was launched into orbit in May 1973. Soon after launch, scientists discovered that part of its protective aluminum shield had torn off, carrying with it a solar panel. NASA sent a three-man crew to meet the station, repair the damage to the solar panel, and install a hastily engineered sun shade. The crew was then able to carry out its mission of astronomical observations and biomedical experiments for 28 days. Two more missions took place before 1979, when *Skylab* descended into Earth's atmosphere and disintegrated despite the efforts of NASA to save it.

Meanwhile, the *Apollo* program drew to a close in the mid-1970s. NASA presented Congress with three possible long-range goals for manned spaceflight: a lunar-orbiting space station, a manned voyage to Mars, and a 50-person Earth-orbiting space station serviced by a fleet of reusable **space shuttles**. Congress rejected all three as too expensive. But NASA officials were determined to win approval for at least one project, the space shuttle. An agreement was made with the Department of Defense (DOD). The DOD would help fund the project in return for use of the shuttle for military projects.

On April 12, 1981, the space shuttle *Columbia* was successfully launched. Twenty-four missions were successfully flown and the American public soon grew used to seeing shuttle launches on **television**. However, on January 28, 1986, the seemingly routine nature of space flight was shattered when the *Challenger* exploded 73 seconds into the flight, killing all seven crew members. An investigation of the disaster revealed that the solid rocket's O-rings had become brittle in the cold weather. They failed to maintain the seal between the fuel tanks, resulting in the explosion.

The next shuttle did not fly again until nearly three years later, after some 400 modifications had been made to its design and its payload (the weight of the crew and supplies it carries) schedule was revised. A replacement for the *Challenger*, the *Endeavour*, saw its first service in 1992.

Soviet Efforts

Unlike the United States, which began the space race with unmanned satellites, the Soviet Union actively pursued manned flight. In 1959 and 1960 a design team headed by Sergei Kolorev constructed several prototypes (first versions) of the first manned spacecraft, *Vostok* ("East"). Soviet scientists also launched several live dogs in *Sputnik* satellites to test the possible stresses that humans might undergo in space.

On January 28, 1986, the seemingly routine nature of space flight was shattered when the Challenger exploded 73 seconds into the flight, killing all seven crew members.

Finally, on April 12, 1961, *Vostok 1* lifted off carrying Yuri Gagarin, the first cosmonaut (astronaut). He circled the planet for 108 minutes before reentering Earth's atmosphere. At about 4 miles (6.4 km) above ground, his ejection seat propelled him from the capsule, and he parachuted to the ground.

The Soviet Union beat the Americans once again when it launched *Voskhod* ("Sunrise"), a three-man spacecraft, in October 1964, well before the first *Gemini* flight. In March 1965 Soviet cosmonaut Alexei Leonov took the first space walk, spending ten minutes outside the *Voskhod* capsule connected to the craft by only telephone and telemetry cables.

The Soviet Union began work on *Soyuz* ("Union"). Problems repeatedly delayed the spacecraft's maiden flight. Finally in April 1967 *Soyuz 1* was launched. Twenty-four hours later, the spacecraft crashed to Earth, with cosmonaut Vladimir Komarov on board. Although Soviet officials denied that design flaws were to blame for the crash, Western analysts concluded that the controls of the craft had failed, causing it to tumble wildly and become tangled in its parachute lines. This disaster halted the Soviet space program. By the time of their first flight following *Soyuz 1* some 18 months later, the Soviets had unofficially conceded defeat in the race for

Sputnik 1 made 4,000 trips around Earth before it gradually lost altitude and disintegrated as it reentered denser atmosphere.

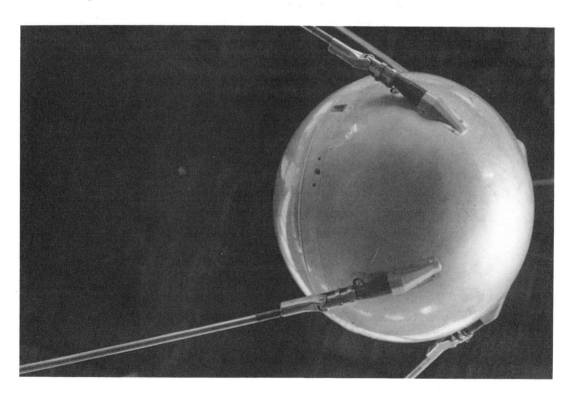

the Moon. They focused instead on establishing the first orbiting **space station**, *Salyut* ("Salute").

The Russians launched their first space station, *Salyut 1*, in April 1971. The station was powered by two solar panels and divided into several different modules, three of which were pressurized for human life support. The three-man crew of *Soyuz 11* successfully entered *Salyut 1* on June 7, 1971. The cosmonauts' highly successful three-week stay set a new record for human endurance in space. But during their reentry into Earth's atmosphere, a cabin seal released prematurely and the spacecraft lost air pressure. The three crew members had not been issued pressure suits and suffocated instantly. As a result of this disaster, the Soviets could not refuel the station. They were forced to allow *Salyut 1* to fall out of its orbit and burn up in reentry. Despite this major setback, the Soviets were eventually able to launch other *Salyut* stations as the decade progressed.

By the early 1980s, the Soviet Union had begun to establish a significant lead in the duration of manned space flight using their *Salyut* stations. Three cosmonauts stayed aloft for 237 days in 1984, nearly three times longer than the American record of 84 days. In 1986 the Soviets launched a new space station, *Mir* ("Peace"), which had less scientific equipment than Salyut but had better accommodations for its cosmonauts. Over the next three years, *Mir* cosmonauts carried out astronomical observations, materials processing and medical experiments, and extensive **photography** of the Earth.

A Joint Venture

By 1970 America had won the race to the Moon. And with relations between the United States and the Soviet Union beginning to improve, a joint space flight seemed possible. A group was formed to study whether a docking between the U.S. *Apollo* and the Soviet *Soyuz* spacecraft was feasible.

Both the Soviets and the Americans had perfect launches on July 15, 1975. After meeting at an agreed-upon spot, the two craft remained locked together in space for two days. The success of the mission raised hopes that further joint missions might be undertaken. But NASA did not have the money, and relations between the countries soured when the Soviets invaded Afghanistan.

The future of manned spaceflight remains uncertain. In the United States the *Challenger* tragedy cost NASA its near-mythic reputation with the American public. Budget problems have caused officials to seriously

With the collapse of the Soviet Union, the "space race"—which drove the achievements of the 1960s—has ended, as Russia struggles to achieve economic stability.

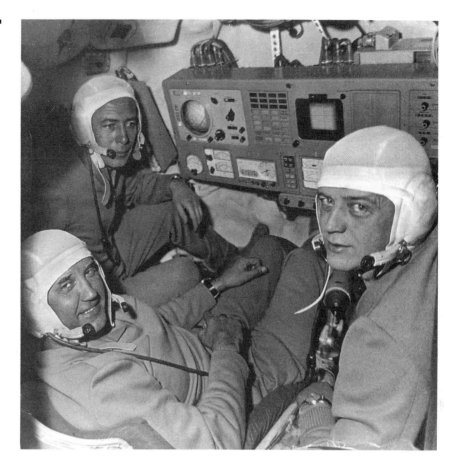

The three-man crew of Soyuz 11 set a new record for human endurance in space. But during their reentry into Earth's atmosphere, a cabin seal released prematurely and the cosmonauts suffocated instantly.

question the funding of multibillion-dollar space programs. And, with the collapse of the Soviet Union, the "space race"—which drove the achievements of the 1960s—has ended as Russia struggles to achieve economic stability.

Facing page: Astronaut Edwin "Buzz" Aldrin walks on the Moon, July 20, 1969. The spacesuits designed for exploration of the Moon had 21 layers and weighed 57 pounds on Earth, less than 10 on the Moon.

⋆⋆ Space equipment

When humans go into space, they face conditions far different from those on Earth. No air or gravity exists. All food and water must be carried along. Temperatures vary greatly. Sudden accelerations and decelerations occur. Sophisticated equipment is required to allow people to survive this hostile environment. Ever since the first *Mercury* flight in 1962, scientists have tried to design space equipment that makes space flight safer and more comfortable for human beings.

The *Mercury* Missions

During the *Mercury* missions in the early 1960s, astronauts depended on a dual life support system, one that maintained temperature and pressure in the spacecraft cabin and one that did the same inside the user's suit.

The early spacesuit was bulky, with many layers that made movement difficult for the astronauts. Air was propelled through the suit and came out through the helmet. Next it passed through a charcoal bed and a chemical scrubber that purified it. The air was then cooled and fed back into the suit. In case of sudden leakage or overuse, **oxygen** from a pair of high-pressure bottles was available.

The *Gemini* Missions

For the *Gemini* spacecraft (built in the mid-1960s), scientists sought to improve the flow of water vapor and temperature control. For those reasons, astronauts used fuel cells, which produced water as a by-product. This helped to prevent the dehydration that had been a major problem on the *Mercury* missions. Temperature was controlled through liquid coolants, electronic equipment, and fuel cells.

The *Gemini* spacesuit had a thinner protective layer and multiple visors. It was also easier to move around in. Oxygen entered at the wearer's waist, circulated, and then exited at the waist. The oxygen supply originated from a container that was much lighter than pressurized bottles. Crews were able to remove their suits for a time and work wearing their long underwear. When the *Gemini* astronauts became the first to leave their spacecraft, a hose was set up to transport oxygen to them. Unfortunately, this system proved inadequate because oxygen supplies were quickly used up.

The *Apollo* Missions

The life-support systems for the *Apollo* missions of the late 1960s to mid-1970s were similar to those of the *Gemini*. However, two new types of spacesuits were designed, one for inside the spacecraft and one for exploration of the **Moon**.

The Moon Suit

The Moon suit had 21 layers. The outer layer was made of **fiberglass** fabric. The next layer was rubber and was pressure-tight. Air pressure was maintained by tubes carrying oxygen that were also used for breathing. Water tubes threaded through the underwear and kept the wearer cool. Both the air pressure and water tubes were connected to a backpack where water, oxygen, and control equipment were stored. Under it all the astronaut wore a urine-collection assembly. On top of it all was a helmet with a thin gold coating to act as a sun visor.

These suits weighed 57 pounds (26 k) on Earth, but only one-sixth as much in the Moon's weaker gravity. It took one hour just to get into them.

The suit worn inside the craft had only six layers, with the outer layer made of fireproof Teflon.

Modern Equipment

Suits

The suits worn by **space shuttle** crews are the safest and the least constrictive of any spacesuit design. They are the result of years of research and testing, and are significantly advanced from the bulky, oppressive suits of the 1960s. They include these improvements:

- liquid-cooled underwear,

- pants and boots with five layers of flexible metallic mylar for heat reflection and protection against micro**meteorites**,

- pleated fabric in places to allow a person to bend or walk,

- a hard-shelled torso (upper body) unit connected by a metal ring to the pants that allows for at least limited turning at the waist, and

- a helmet and gloves attached by locking devices to prevent them from accidentally coming loose.

Food

Inside the spacecraft is equipment necessary for drinking, eating, sleeping, going to the bathroom, and exercising. Before the early *Mercury* flights, there was concern whether eating would be affected by zero-gravity. Scientists did not know whether people would be able to swallow solid food or if it would get stuck in their

Mercury astronaut John Glenn became the first American to orbit the Earth on February 20, 1962. Equipment aboard today's space shuttles is much more sophisticated and comfortable than on the early Mercury missions.

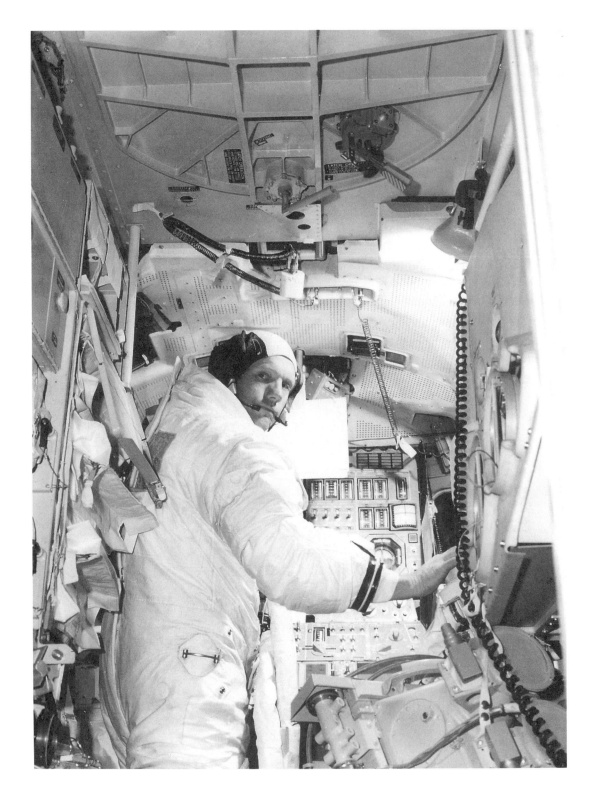

throats. As a result, the early astronauts ate pureed foods, such as apple-sauce, out of squeeze tubes.

In later *Mercury* flights, after scientists realized the only problem was keeping food on the spoon, astronauts ate from plastic sacks of freeze-dried foods that could be injected with water. As interior space in the craft increased, the crews ate better and more varied meals. Today, shuttle crews might have bacon and eggs for breakfast, spaghetti and meatballs for lunch, and barbecued beef for dinner.

Elimination

The early astronauts had to use bags to urinate and defecate in. Now shuttles have space toilets that look a little like those on airplanes (cost: $3 million each). What is different are the foot restraints, handholds, and waist restraints that help maintain a seal between the user and the seat. A fan located under the toilet seat provides a downward air flow that forces the fluids and solid wastes into collection receptacles.

Bathing

Skylab (mid-1970s) was equipped with a shower in a folding stall that relied on a vacuum system to dispose of the water. It was difficult to use and it leaked. Shuttles fly for a much shorter time, so they have no shower facilities. Instead, crew members take sponge-baths, as they did on the *Mercury, Gemini,* and *Apollo* missions.

Exercise and Sleep

Exercise on long missions is accomplished with treadmills, stationary bicycles, and special exercises that stimulate the circulation of blood through the legs. Today's larger spacecraft have enclosures much like sleeping bags for the crew to use so they can sleep unstrapped without floating.

Equipment aboard today's space shuttles is much more sophisticated and comfortable than on the early *Mercury* missions. As space technology advances and flights travel farther and last for longer periods, scientists will design devices and equipment that protect as well as enhance the space experience for human beings. One such invention is the Safer (simplified aid for extravehicular activity rescue), a jet pack tested by U.S. shuttle pilots during 1994 space flights. A pilot wearing a jet pack can use the device to guide himself or herself back to the spacecraft in case of an accident.

Opposite page: Neil Armstrong aboard Apollo 11. The spacesuit designed for inside the spacecraft had only six layers.

⋆⋆⋆ Space probe

A space probe is a spacecraft that carries instruments (instead of astronauts) such as photographic equipment. It is designed to explore outer space or heavenly bodies other than Earth. Space probe voyages last many years.

The former Soviet Union was the first to launch a space probe, *Luna 1*, in 1959. It missed the Moon by 3,728 miles (5,998 km). *Luna 3*, launched the same year, gave us our first pictures of the far side of the Moon.

The former Soviet Union scored another first when it soft-landed (as opposed to crash-landed) *Luna 9* on the Moon's surface in 1966. *Luna 9* transmitted television pictures for three days. The United States followed suit with the *Surveyor* series, soft-landing a capsule four months after *Luna 9* had landed. The *Surveyor* had more sophisticated landing capability and sent back more than 11,000 pictures.

Pioneer 10 took this photo of Jupiter and its famous Red Spot before it continued into interstellar space, the first man-made object to leave the solar system.

Mariner and Venera Series

Next the two nations turned their attention to Mars and Venus. The United States's *Mariner* series accomplished the following:

- came within 21,594 miles (34,745 km) of Venus after its launch in 1962,

- returned the first close-up photographs of Mars when it approached within 6,118 miles (9,844 km) of the red planet in 1965,

- photographed the clouds of Venus before sending back the first pictures of the moon-like Mercury,

- flew within 3,400 miles (5,470 km) of Mars in 1969, showing a surface of craters, and

- settled into orbit around Mars in 1971, sending back more than 7,000 pictures of the planet. Photos revealed huge canyons that dwarfed the Grand Canyon, monstrous volcanoes, and what appeared to be dried-out beds of ancient rivers.

A space probe carries cameras, telescopes, and radio transmitters to send deep space information to people back on Earth.

The former Soviet Union focused more on Venus. *Venera 7* actually landed on Venus in 1970. Cameras on *Venera 9* and *Venera 10* sent back startling photos of a harsh, rocky world.

Viking Series

Viking 1 and *Viking 2* reached Mars in 1976, sending back thousands of high-quality photographs. Special equipment known as landers scooped up Martian soil to analyze for any indications of the existence of life (results were inconclusive). The landers collected weather reports, while overhead, the *Viking* orbiters mapped much of the Martian surface.

Pioneer and Ranger Series

The National Aeronautics and Space Administration (NASA) tried unsuccessfully to reach the Moon during the 1960s with the early *Pioneer* series. It next launched the *Ranger* series, which was unsuccessful until the last three—*Ranger 7, Ranger 8,* and *Ranger 9*—took more than 17,000 pictures of the Moon starting in 1963.

Next, *Pioneer 10* and *Pioneer 11* took close-up photos of Jupiter and its famous Red Spot. *Pioneer 11* went on to Saturn, while *Pioneer 10*

E u r e k a !

continued into interstellar space, the first man-made object to leave the solar system.

Voyager Series

Probably the most famous space probes were *Voyager 1* and *Voyager 2*, launched by the United States in 1977. Once every 176 years the giant planets—Jupiter, Neptune, Saturn, and Uranus—align themselves in such a way that a spacecraft launched from Earth to Jupiter might be able to visit the other three planets on the same mission. *Voyager 1* and *Voyager 2* were able to take advantage of this opportunity. They:

- sent back the first clear photos of Jupiter's Red Spot and of Saturn's rings,
- sent back new information about the motion, composition, and origin of Uranus and its moons, and
- discovered new moons, rings, arcs within rings, intriguing cloud features, and an unexpectedly skewed (tipped) magnetic field on Neptune.

Magellan and *Galileo*

To get a better idea of what Venus was like, the United States launched *Magellan* from the space shuttle *Atlantis* in 1989. *Magellan* is sending back pictures of impact craters and volcanoes, trying to help us understand the geological history of Venus.

After many delays, the American probe *Galileo* was launched in 1989. *Galileo* encountered Venus in late 1991, swung once more past Earth in late 1992, and should arrive near Jupiter in December 1995. There it will drop a probe into the clouds above Jupiter and continue to circle the giant planet, providing information about it and its moons.

While the Soviet Union, which dissolved in 1991, no longer sends up probes, the Europeans have entered the picture. In 1986 the European space probe *Giotto* flew near Halley's comet and sent back photos.

⋆⋆ Space shuttle

The shuttle is a **rocket**-boosted spacecraft that carries satellites and **space probes**. The shuttle can make repeated space flights.

Opposite page: Scale model of a Voyager *spacecraft.* Voyager 1 *and* 2 *were able to study Jupiter, Neptune, Saturn, and Uranus on the same mission.*

A space shuttle is a rocket-boosted spacecraft that carries satellites and space probes. A shuttle can make repeated space flights.

Reusable Spacecraft Needed

The rockets used on America's first spacecraft could be launched only once, so every space flight involved a tremendous waste of resources and materials. Researchers at the National Aeronautics and Space Administration (NASA) decided to try to build a reusable spacecraft. Spacecraft design engineer Maxim Faget and a team of 20 top scientists came up with the shuttle.

The craft was 122 feet long with a wingspan of 78 feet, a triangular-shaped wing for greater efficiency high in the atmosphere, and a throw-away tank and solid-propellant boosters.

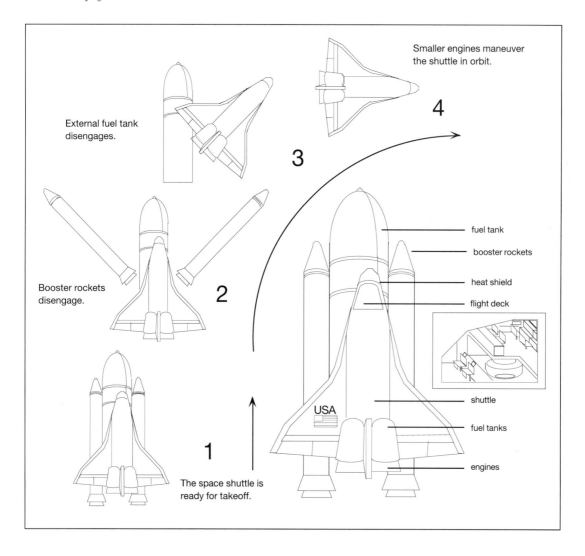

Smaller engines maneuver the shuttle in orbit.

External fuel tank disengages.

3

4

Booster rockets disengage.

2

fuel tank

booster rockets

heat shield

flight deck

shuttle

USA

fuel tanks

engines

1

The space shuttle is ready for takeoff.

NASA optimistically predicted 570 shuttle flights for the 1980s and 1990s. NASA's original plan was to use the shuttle to carry people and supplies to a planned space station. A number of other shuttle advantages were touted: the shuttle was a money-saving, reusable replacement for NASA's old-style launch vehicles. In addition, a successful shuttle could make money by flying missions for industries and other nations for a fee. A shuttle could help build industrial operations in space, where zero-gravity conditions allow precision manufacturing.

Enterprise and *Columbia*

The first shuttle was named *Enterprise* for the starship of the same name in *Star Trek*. Tests carried out in 1977 proved that the heaviest glider ever flown (150,000 pounds [68,040 kg]) could glide safely to a landing on Earth. In 1981 the *Columbia* became the first shuttle to orbit Earth, returning safely to Earth 54 hours after liftoff.

The fleet of space shuttles was grounded for 32 months after Challenger *exploded 73 seconds after launch.*

What Can a Shuttle Do?

The shuttle uses an arm that can manipulate large objects either to lift them out of the cargo bay or to retrieve them from space. Astronauts use a manned maneuvering unit (MMU), which allows them to fly into space near the shuttle without being attached to the shuttle. With these devices, crews can retrieve and repair disabled satellites, or retrieve them for future re-launch.

American space shuttles are launched vertically like any other rocket. They use their own engines and two attached rocket boosters to blast into space. After their fuel is used, the rocket boosters drop back into the atmosphere, where they burn up before reaching Earth. To reenter the Earth's atmosphere, the shuttle turns around, brakes with its engines, and descends like a glider. It lands on special three-mile long runways in Florida or California as if it were an airplane.

Challenger, Discovery, Atlantis

From April 1981 to January 1986 the shuttle fleet—*Challenger, Discovery,* and *Atlantis*—flew 24 consecutive successful missions. The shuttles delivered 28 non-military satellites to orbit. Spacelab, a unit containing equipment for scientific experiments, was carried by the fleet on four flights.

Disaster

The shuttle program encountered disaster on the cold morning of January 28, 1986. *Challenger* exploded 73 seconds after launch, due to a faulty seal in its solid rocket booster. All seven crew members died as a result. The fleet of shuttles was grounded for 32 months while more than 400 changes in the shuttle's construction were made.

NASA has since put the shuttles back into flight. A replacement for *Challenger,* called *Endeavour,* has been built, but no additional shuttles are planned for the time being.

⋆⋆ Space station

Space stations are large spacecraft designed for long-term space orbit or travel. Astronauts are carried to them on smaller craft to live and work for several weeks or months at a time. Supplies and new crews arrive in ferry spacecraft that link up with the space station.

Soviet Space Stations

Salyut

The Soviet Union launched the first space station, *Salyut 1*, in April 1971. Its first crew arrived aboard the *Soyuz 24* in June. At the forward end of *Salyut* was a docking port and transfer compartment to link the station with the craft carrying the crew.

The crew of the *Salyut* carried out astronomical research, plant growth experiments, and Earth observations. On its way home, a seal broke aboard the ferry craft *Soyuz 24*. The crew died instantly.

The Soviets experienced two more failures before launching *Salyut 3* in June 1974. One crew stayed aboard for 16 days. Later *Salyut* stations had more solar power, allowing more experiments and longer missions. The Soviets perfected the science of resupplying *Salyut* with unmanned, automatic vehicles. These **robot** ships brought fresh supplies of oxygen, food, water, and scientific equipment.

All orbiting spacecraft experience a similar problem when their orbit starts to decay. Without intervention, the craft will start to fall into Earth's gravity. The *Salyuts* solved this problem by using re-startable engines to push them into higher orbits when necessary. These improvements allowed the cosmonauts (the Russian term for astronaut) to stay in space for longer and longer periods. In 1984 a crew stayed in a *Salyut* station for 237 days, a world record.

Mir

A new space station, *Mir,* was launched in February 1986. It had more docking ports and improved accommodations for crew members. The same year, the Soviets carried out the first successful transfer of cosmonauts between stations, from *Salyut 7* to *Mir.*

In three years, the *Mir* cosmonauts completed nine "space walks" and carried out numerous scientific experiments. Future modules (pieces) to be added to *Mir* were planned, but the breakup of the Soviet Union put a halt to manned Russian space flights for the immediate future.

U.S. Space Stations

Skylab

The American space station *Skylab* was a two-story complex with enough room for three astronauts. The bottom section consisted of a ward

Space stations are large spacecraft designed for long-term space orbit or travel.

*A U.S. Customs
official in San
Francisco examines
the largest piece of
Skylab. The chunk
of debris was
shipped to the
United States from
Australia after the
craft fell through
Earth's atmosphere
into the Indian
Ocean in July 1979.*

room (recreation and dining area), sleep compartments, and a bathroom. The upper deck contained a workshop about the same size as a small three-bedroom house. Large solar panels powered the station, and a thin aluminum shield protected against micrometeorites and excessive solar heat.

Soon after launch on May 14, 1973, *Skylab* encountered trouble. Part of the protective shield tore off, carrying with it one of the solar energy panels. The station was now seriously underpowered and was vulnerable to overheating from the **Sun.** Eleven days later, a three-person crew was launched to meet the station. They first worked outside the station to repair the damage to the solar panel and to install a sun shade. For the next 28 days the *Skylab* crew continued with its original mission, observing the Sun, photographing the Earth, and carrying out biomedical experiments.

A second crew was ferried to *Skylab* in July 1973. For 59 days the crew conducted experiments in biology, space medicine, solar physics, and

astrophysics. A final crew boarded *Skylab* in November 1973, remaining in space for 84 days, observing a solar flare and conducting research.

In 1979 *Skylab*'s orbit faltered. Plans were made for a new **space shuttle** to attach a booster rocket to the *Skylab,* carrying it to a higher orbit. But before the shuttle was ready, an outburst of sunspots caused Earth's atmosphere to expand and slowed the station down. It plunged back into Earth's atmosphere in July and burned up before it could be saved. No one was aboard at the time.

Freedom

A new and ambitious space station called *Freedom* is being built. It is a joint effort by the United States, Canada, Japan, and ten European nations. It will take four years and twenty-six space shuttle flights to complete. Its purpose is to find out if humans can live for long periods of time in space. It will also provide a taking-off place for interplanetary travel. The first space shuttle mission to carry equipment for *Freedom* is set for October 1997.

⋆⋆ Space telescope

Scientists have learned that a majority of objects in space—from cold planets and stars to extremely hot galaxies and **quasars**—emit infrared rays. Infrared rays lie outside the color spectrum at the red end. This radiation is absorbed by water vapor in the Earth's atmosphere, protecting us. But the vapor also makes our ground **telescopes** useless in gathering information about this radiation.

Ground telescopes have traditionally been located on mountains, where the atmosphere is thinnest, in an effort to overcome atmospheric interference. This solution, however, has not been very satisfying to astronomers. Space telescopes were devised to fulfill the dreams of astronomers for optical telescopes placed above Earth's distorting atmosphere. Optical telescopes use special lenses to make distant objects appear closer and clearer.

Astronomers are keenly interested in **ultraviolet radiation.** In the 1970s *Apollo* and *Skylab* carried small ultraviolet telescopes into space. The *International Ultraviolet Explorer* (*IUE*) satellite was launched in 1979, and it conducted some of the best ultraviolet work to date. It was

Space telescopes were devised to fulfill the dreams of astronomers: optical telescopes placed above Earth's distorting atmosphere.

E u r e k a !

used to study supernovas as well as to produce very high quality photographs of spectra (light and energy waves).

X-rays and **gamma rays** are also of major interest to astronomers.
X-rays provide information about the violent upheavals that create and
destroy stars. Several small satellites launched during the 1970s looked
closely at X-ray and gamma ray radiation. They revealed hundreds of previously unknown sources of this radiation, including at least one black
hole. Beginning in 1977 and throughout the rest of that decade, several
High Energy Astrophysical Observatories (*HEAO*) satellites were
launched, carrying an assortment of X-ray and gamma ray detectors that
provided readings on even the weakest sources of radiation. The *Small
Astronomy Satellite* (*SAS*) was also launched in the late 1970s to detect
gamma ray sources in the Milky Way, the galaxy in which our solar system is located.

In 1983 Great Britain, the Netherlands, and the United States shared
in the development of the *Infrared Astronomical Satellite* (*IRAS*).
Launched on January 25, 1983, *IRAS* operated for only ten months, but it
surveyed almost the entire sky. It discovered many galaxies, glowing with
infrared radiation, barely detectable with Earth-based optical telescopes.
The satellite also collected an immense amount of information about the
infrared universe.

The 1990s have seen increased activity in exploration of the universe.
In 1990 the European Space Agency launched *ROSAT,* a satellite designed
to capture sharp X-ray images and to detect undiscovered ultraviolet wavelengths. Since its mission began, *ROSAT* has uncovered what could be a
new class of very bright stars and supernova remnants. The National Aeronautics and Space Administration (NASA) has also initiated its own programs: Gamma Ray Observatory (GRO); Advanced X-ray Astrophysics
Facility (AXAF); and Space Infrared Telescope Facility (SIRTF). Perhaps
the most well-known NASA project is the Hubble Space Telescope (HST).

The Hubble Space Telescope

The HST was launched by the **space shuttle** *Discovery* on April 24,
1990. Its job was to see farther into deep space than any previous telescope.
Unfortunately, a slight imperfection in one of its mirrors prevented the
complicated, $1.5 billion device from focusing properly. A later shuttle
mission was able to do repairs on HST, bringing it up to near 90 percent
efficiency. The shuttle crew replaced four of the six malfunctioning gyro-
scopes that helped focus the mirror, and added a co-star feature to the

*Opposite page: The
Hubble Space
Telescope is
deployed from a
space shuttle.*

mirror itself. The co-star acts as a pair of eyeglasses would, helping the HST produce a sharper image.

The repairs to the HST paid off. In July 1994 the telescope took hundreds of pictures as 20 large chunks of the comet Shoemaker-Levy 9 smashed into Jupiter. The images helped astronomers learn more about Jupiter's composition and about comets and celestial crashes.

The HST was planned to operate for 15 years, and designed to be serviced every three to five years. The routine service is needed because the HST experiences instabilities in each orbit (it circles Earth every 96 minutes) that jar and shift its delicate instruments.

⋆⋆ Spectroscopy

A star's spectrum. Astronomers observe the spectra of distant stars through a spectroscope to determine their chemical makeup.

Scientists use spectroscopy to learn about the makeup of distant stars and the nature of chemical elements here on Earth. Anyone who has ever used a prism to split a beam of white light into its component colors has practiced spectroscopy. Spectroscopy is a technique that separates light according to its frequencies, or wavelengths. In our prism example, the many frequencies within a beam of white light are scattered to reveal a spectrum. By examining which colors within that spectrum are brighter or dimmer, a scientist learns about the source of the white light.

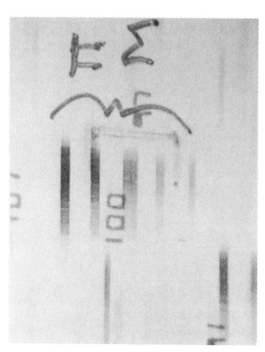

Many scientists, including **Isaac Newton**, experimented with prisms. It was physicist Joseph von Fraunhofer who first applied spectroscopy to analytical science. In 1814, while examining some old lenses, he discovered that the spectrum of the **Sun**'s light, until this time thought to be continuous, was actually interrupted by hundreds of dark lines. Others claimed that the lines were caused by imperfections in the lenses, but Fraunhofer believed that they were characteristic of the light itself. Unfortunately, the technology did not exist to examine the phenomenon any further.

In 1859 German scientists Robert Bunsen and Gustav Kirchhoff designed a spectrometer that could record the spectra of light. They found that when elements were superheated, they emit

The Color Spectrum

White light is actually a combination of light waves of different colors and lengths. As white light enters a prism, it is bent slightly. More importantly, each color is bent to a different degree from the rest. This causes the light to spread out, forming what we call the color spectrum.

The colors in the color spectrum always appear in the same order: red, orange, yellow, green, blue, indigo, and violet. (You can remember the order by using ROY G BIV—a mnemonic to aid memory retention.) Red is the longest light wave and violet is the shortest. Longer wave lengths are bent more sharply by the prism than the shorter waves.

Scientists use spectroscopy to learn about the makeup of distant stars and the nature of chemical elements here on Earth.

a particular color of light. (Bunsen invented the **Bunsen burner** for this purpose). When they examined the elements' lights through a prism, they found that each element had a unique spectrum, like a spectroscopic fingerprint. Using their new device, Bunsen and Kirchhoff catalogued the spectra of all the known elements, plus the two new elements they discovered—cesium and rubidium.

Use in Astronomy

Astronomers observe the spectra of distant stars through a spectroscope to determine their chemical makeup. The first scientist to make a systematic spectroscopic study of the heavens was the Italian Pietro Angelo Secchi, who examined the spectra of nearly 4,000 stars during the late 1860s.

Spectroscopy is not confined to use with visible light. In 1912 the father-and-son team of William Henry Bragg and William Lawrence Bragg examined the spectral patterns of **X-rays** using a diffraction grating rather than a prism. Diffraction gratings use close-set grooves to disperse (spread out) the frequencies within light. Since X-rays have much shorter wavelengths than do light rays, it was important to find a diffraction grating that had grooves set very close together, much closer than any machine could cut them. The Braggs found the ideal natural diffraction grating in a crystal, whose layered atomic structure diffused the X-rays perfectly.

The Braggs' effort gave the world a greater understanding of how X-rays work. It also served as the cornerstone for the creation of a new science, X-ray crystallography. This method was used most successfully to synthesize (artificially create) **penicillin**, **vitamin B$_{12}$**, and **insulin**.

See also **Light, diffraction of**

⋆⋆ Split-brain functioning

For thousands of years scientists, doctors, and even poets have explored the workings of the human brain. In many ways, the brain is still unmapped territory. In fact, an important finding was made as recently as the 1960s. The surprising breakthrough came when a scientist realized that the two halves of the brain perform different functions and can act independently of each other.

Many paired body parts, such as the eyes, kidneys, and lungs, do the same job. Thus it is usually possible to live normally with only one of these parts. For example, if a person closes his left eye he can still see with the right eye, and if a person has a kidney removed, the remaining kidney performs for both. So Roger W. Sperry was astounded to discover that the two halves (or hemispheres) of the brain were so very different. Sperry was a neurophysiologist, a scientist who studies how the nervous system works in the human body.

Work of Roger Sperry

Sperry came by his discovery only after years of study. In the 1950s he had been working at the University of Chicago with Paul Weiss, a developmental biologist (a scientist who studies growth and change in human beings). Together they had been studying the corpus callosum, the narrow bundle of some 200 million neurons that connect the two halves of the brain. With help from graduate student Ronald Myers, Sperry removed the corpus callosum brain tissue from an animal. Through a series of tests, Sperry and his colleagues learned that each half of the animal's brain could act independently.

Similar tests on monkeys and chimpanzees confirmed the earlier results, but Sperry and Myers wondered if the human brain would act in the same way. To study this, Sperry turned to research done on epileptic patients in the 1940s. An epileptic suffers from seizures or fits that are caused by misfires in the brain's **nervous system**. In the 1940s two neurosurgeons, faced with a patient who suffered from crippling epilepsy,

Neurophysiologist Roger Sperry won the 1981 Nobel Prize in Medicine for his work in the field of split-brain functioning.

severed (cut) the patient's corpus callosum after all other attempts to control the patient's seizures had failed. Thereafter, the seizures occurred only in half the brain. The operation had little impact on the patient's personality, intelligence, or mental ability, but it did cut down the seizure rate.

Sperry used these studies as a basis for his research at the California Institute of Technology with graduate student Michael S. Gazzaniga. Sperry studied an epileptic patient who had shown significant improvement when his corpus callosum was severed. Repeating the tests he had conducted earlier with animals, Sperry used flash cards and covered the patient's eyes. He observed the way the patient saw and remembered images. The patient showed that he was able to view flash cards with his right eye. But even though his body language and other nonverbal cues told the researchers that he had seen flash cards with his left eye, the patient was unable to say what he had seen with his left eye.

Sperry and Gazzaniga thus answered the question of the function of the corpus callosum: Things that people see with their left eye are registered in their right brain hemisphere. This perception is sent through the corpus callosum to the left hemisphere, where the ability to make a spoken response is lodged. Sperry concluded that the corpus callosum is insignificant in creating any added functioning dependency (reliance) between the two separate brain halves. The real function of the corpus callosum is to allow communication between the two hemispheres.

Further tests continued to confirm the split-brain functioning makeup. Each half of the brain could function independently, but one half showed certain strengths over the other. For example, the right half of the brain proved to be superior in spatial perceptions (observing how things relate to or occupy space) while the left brain was clearly superior in logic and verbal and mathematical skills. The right brain/left brain theory received media attention in the 1980s when many popular books were published about how to tap into the unexplored creative or analytical side of the brain.

Things that people see with their left eye are registered in their right brain hemisphere.

⋆⋆ Stapler

The stapler is a necessary piece of equipment in any office. It is used to temporarily bind together two or more separate sheets of paper. Its invention in 1868 is credited to Charles H. Gould. There is little difference between Gould's stapler and the desk model we use today. Both have

U-shaped wires placed in a channel (passage). The wires are forced into paper by a blade, which breaks off individual wires from the strip. A small metal piece under the papers bends the wire flat.

Automatic versions of the stapler have been developed to fill the needs of today's faster-paced offices and factories. The basic principle remains the same as Gould's stapler, but each new version is able to complete different tasks. For example, industrial staplers are used in furniture making, upholstering, packaging, and magazine binding. Some stapling machines, called tackers, use the power of compressed air to drive staples into material without bending them. A related variation is the hog ring machine, a device that bends staple legs into a tight ring around the twisted neck of a bag. This is used to securely close filled sacks and bags without piercing the material itself. Some frozen chicken and turkey bags are sealed with hog rings.

Star cluster

Star clusters are systems made up of tens of thousands to trillions of stars.

When you look up at the sky on a clear night, you are not looking at a random scattering of stars. Rather, you are looking at star systems, stars bound to each other by **gravity**. A **binary star** system contains two stars rotating around each other. About half of all stars are members of binary systems.

Star clusters are systems made up of tens of thousands to trillions of stars. There are two basic types: "globular" clusters and "open" clusters.

Cluster Types

Globular clusters are nearly spherical (ball-shaped) star systems with the greatest concentration of stars near their centers. In fact, there are so many stars at the center that individual members cannot be distinguished—only a continuous glow is visible. But there is plenty of space between these stars. In one of the closer globulars, M13 in the Hercules constellation, more than 30,000 stars have been counted. There may be many more stars that are too faint to be seen.

Opposite page: More than 100 globular clusters have been spotted in the Milky Way. They are far from the Sun and surround the galaxy's spiral arms in a great halo.

More than 100 globular clusters have been spotted in the Milky Way, the galaxy in which our **solar system** is located. They are far from the **Sun** and surround the galaxy's spiral arms in a great halo.

Open star clusters, in contrast to the globulars, are relatively loose groupings of stars. They contain far fewer members than the globulars,

E u r e k a !

have no great concentration at their core, and lack symmetry (balance). They are located within the Milky Way galaxy, so they are often called galactic clusters.

It is believed open clusters originated within the spiral arms of the Milky Way. More than 1,000 open clusters have been identified, but a great many more may go undetected because of interstellar matter that blocks our view of the Milky Way's plane. One of the most famous of the open clusters is the Pleiades cluster in the Taurus constellation.

Beyond the Milky Way

Star clusters are certainly not limited to the Milky Way galaxy. In 1924 U.S. astronomer Edwin Powell Hubble identified globular clusters in what, at the time, were believed to be nebula within the Milky Way. Nebula are clouds of dust particles and hydrogen gas. He discovered that the distance from Earth to these globulars, and the nebula in which they were located, was so great that these globulars had to be entirely separate galaxies. Thus Hubble proved that the Milky Way was not the only galaxy in the universe.

⋆⋆ Steady-state theory

The steady-state theory, one of the most popular explanations of the origin of the universe ever devised, says that the universe looks the same everywhere and forever.

Over the centuries, there have been many theories that try to explain the origins of the universe. One of the most popular is called the steady-state theory. It was proposed in 1948 and had many supporters until it was finally abandoned in the 1960s.

The theory was first proposed by Thomas Gold and Hermann Bondi. They suggested that the structure of the universe is homogeneous. That is, the universe is the same everywhere, no matter where in the universe you are located. They called this theory the cosmological principle. Cosmology is the study of the structure and evolution of the universe.

They went on to suggest that the universe was not only the same from everywhere, but also from "every-when." So, the universe should look the same not only from all locations, but at all times, past, present and future.

But others observed that the universe was not consistent. For example, in 1929 American astronomer Edwin Powell Hubble found that the universe was expanding, and the galaxies were all moving away from each other.

To account for such observations, supporters of Gold and Bondi's theory suggested that as the galaxies spread apart, new matter was created in the empty space left behind. This matter became new galaxies just like the old galaxies, and so the cosmos remained steady.

Many astronomers, including Fred Hoyle, adopted the steady-state theory enthusiastically. It was simple and had balance. The universe was seen as infinite, unchanging, and everlasting. Unfortunately, the theory had a number of problems.

Problems With Steady-State Theory

The most significant problem with the theory was the idea of continuous creation. According to the steady-state theory, matter was being *constantly* created out of nothing. For Hoyle and others like him, it was far easier to accept the steady-state theory, where *a little bit* of matter was being continuously created over time, than it was to accept the opposing theory, the **big bang,** which held that *all the matter in the universe* was created instantaneously.

And, if the steady-state theory were correct, astronomers should see some galaxies made up of very old, evolved stars while other galaxies contained mostly new stars. This was not the case. All the galaxies had stars of all ages in them.

Proponents of both theories argued for years. Finally, in 1963, the steady-state theory began to crumble when Maarten Schmidt discovered **quasars**. Steady-state cosmology could not account for these strange objects, which are thought to be distant galaxies. If matter were being created continuously, one would expect to see quasars spread evenly everywhere.

In 1964 Arno Penzias and Robert W. Wilson detected the background microwave radiation that had been predicted by the big bang theory. The steady-state theory was abandoned. Furthermore, the popular big bang theory has been reevaluated and is being modified into the inflationary theory of creation, which suggests that the universe expanded much faster at first than it does now. This concept of accelerated expansion allows for the formation of the planets and stars in the universe today.

⋆⋆ Stealth aircraft

The term "stealth aircraft" was first introduced to the American public in the 1980s and 1990s, when the U.S. Air Force first allowed a glimpse of

In 1963 the steady-state theory began to crumble when Maarten Schmidt discovered quasars. Steady-state cosmology could not account for these strange objects.

*The
development of
radar at the
beginning of
World War II
significantly
changed air
strategy.*

its highly classified F-117A fighter and B-2 bomber. But these **aircraft** and the cutting-edge technology involved in their design were the result of a process that began during World War I (1914-18).

That war's top pilots understood the importance of surprise, of spotting and attacking the enemy before being detected. The most successful strategy involved maneuvering into position so as to be silhouetted against the sun before attacking. The sun created a blind spot so the attack airplane was harder to see. To make their craft less visible in that position, the Germans covered some of their planes with heavy cellophane skins. The cellophane allowed sunlight to pass through the plane. This new material, however, failed to hold up under the stress of flying and was soon abandoned. But the idea of making planes invisible continued to fire the imagination of aeronautical engineers.

In the 1930s, planes could fly high enough and fast enough to avoid being seen, so not much emphasis was placed on stealth design. One significant exception, however, was the American P-38 Lightning, designed by Lockheed. This plane was difficult to see because of its smaller side and front profiles.

The development of **radar** at the beginning of World War II (1939-45) significantly changed air strategy. Airplanes previously too high to be seen could now be sought out by land-based radar and destroyed. Aircraft designers began to equip planes with radar and devices to jam or distort enemy signals. Some bombers even dropped chaff, which were thin metal strips that confused the radar and disguised the bomber's location. "Electronic warfare," as it came to be known, escalated dramatically during that war.

The escalation continued with the introduction of the **jet engine** in the 1950s. Aircraft, particularly bombers, grew larger and more complicated. And, as radar grew more sophisticated and diversified, attack missions became more dangerous. Such missions often involved a wide range of aircraft, and the purpose of some of these aircraft was only to create an electronic smoke screen. By the end of the Vietnam War (1965-73), the danger and expense of relying on electronic warfare forced the United States military to seek an alternative. It eventually turned to Lockheed, the company that had designed some of the military's most successful reconnaissance aircraft. Reconnaissance aircraft conduct inspections, often of enemy territory.

Lockheed, with the help of the Central Intelligence Agency (CIA), set about building a spy plane that could perform in an air battle but would not be easily detected otherwise.

The U-2

The group eventually produced the U-2, first flown in 1955. The U-2 proved the value of designing with stealth in mind. It had a small size, slender profile, and black paint that absorbed radar probes rather than reflecting them back. Lockheed followed the U-2 with the A-12, which eventually evolved into the SR-71 Blackbird, one of the most distinctive airplanes ever built. Its wing-mounted engines and slim fuselage (body) created a slender side profile. Its smooth body, boasting few straight angles, made it difficult to detect with radar. Designers also used a radar-absorbent **plastic** material on the wing's leading edges and control surfaces.

Despite these advances, however, reconnaissance planes flown by pilots were largely discontinued after the famous incident in which a U-2 was shot down over the Soviet Union in 1960. The United States military then turned to spy satellites and unmanned drones (radio-controlled airplanes).

Lockheed and the U.S. Air Force next turned their attention to a plane made of a material that would be transparent to radar. (Instead of absorbing radar, the radar would be unable to see this new material.) The project was officially designated "Have Blue," but it was unofficially referred to as "Project Harvey," after the invisible rabbit in the 1950s movie, *Harvey*.

The F-117A

The members of "Have Blue" had to overcome a wide range of obstacles. The presence of an aircraft in flight is betrayed by many different signs (noise, for example). Designers covered up many of these telltale signals by placing the plane's weapons and engines inside and avoiding designs that made an easily tracked shape such as steep vertical slopes, large flat surfaces, and straight lines. To eliminate hot spots that could be picked up by infrared detectors, the exhaust was deflected upward. Advanced radar-absorbent materials were manufactured and used as the skin of the prototype (first version). These efforts produced the F-117A, finally revealed to the public in 1990, thirteen years after its first flight. The F-117A proved its worth in the Persian Gulf War of 1991, when it successfully completed missions against Iraq's most heavily defended targets without suffering damage.

The B-2

Along with the F-117A, the most advanced stealth aircraft yet designed is the B-2 bomber. Northrop Corporation designed the B-2 with

Reconnaissance planes flown by pilots were largely discontinued after the famous incident in which a U-2 was shot down over the Soviet Union in 1960.

a large wing over which the weight of the craft is distributed, thus hiding the cockpit and engines in the wing. The almost perfectly flat bomber with its radar-absorbing skin diffracts (turns away) most incoming radar waves. Several B-2s have been manufactured, but the enormous costs involved led some U.S. government officials in the early 1990s to reevaluate the project.

⁺⁺ Steam engine

Steam engines were one of the earliest and most important inventions to convert one form of energy to another.

Machines were invented to make the work of humans easier or safer. Simple machines (such as levers, pulleys, inclined planes, screws, wheels and axles, and wedges) have been in use for thousands of years. Complex machines, while they are more recent inventions, rely largely on combinations and refinements of these basic machines.

Machines need energy to function, whether it is animal or human muscle, wind or water currents, or heat-generated energy, such as steam. Steam engines were one of the earliest and most important inventions to convert one form of energy to another. Some historians even credit the steam engine with making possible Europe's industrial revolution, which occurred during the late eighteenth and the nineteenth centuries.

Moving Toward Steam

One of the first steam-powered machines was built in 1698 by the English military engineer Thomas Savery. His invention, designed to pump water out of coal mines, was known as the Miner's Friend. The Miner's Friend used suction to start the movement of the water from the mine floor. Savery's machine, which had no moving parts, consisted of a simple boiler, a steam chamber whose valves were located on the surface, and a pipe leading to the water in the flooded levels of the mine below.

Some historians credit the steam engine with making possible Europe's industrial revolution.

The French-born British physicist Denis Papin improved Savery's pump by adding pistons to create water movement. These attempts were crude and missed the power of the steam itself. Instead these inventors used the condensation (water) created by the steam to do the job.

Further advancements on the Savery pump were made in 1712 by the British engineer Thomas Newcomen. With his assistant, John Calley, Newcomen became the first to harness power by setting a moving piston inside a cylinder, a technique still in use today. Newcomen's design was important because the motion created allowed the engine to keep running on its own power. Newcomen's engine is called an "atmospheric engine" and was a forerunner of the higher-pressure steam engines to come.

In the 1720s, the German inventor Jacob Leupold designed a remarkably advanced engine that eliminated the condensation and vacuum steps of this process. Leupold's design called for two symmetrical (balanced) cylinders that moved in opposition to create a continuous power source. The engine was apparently never built, however, probably because of limitations in the materials available and the then-current levels of craftsmanship.

Watt's Breakthrough

Scottish engineer James Watt contributed most to the development of the modern steam engine. He sealed the engine's cylinder and installed steam valves on both ends. These design changes made his engines more efficient because less heat was lost during operation.

Watt also was responsible for an even more impressive innovation: attaching a flywheel to the engine. A flywheel is a heavy disc that rotates on a shaft, the momentum of which gives almost uniform rotational speed. Flywheels accomplished two tasks. First, a large flywheel allowed the engine to run more smoothly by creating a more constant load. Second, flywheels converted the conventional back-and-forth power stroke into a circular motion that could be adapted easily to run machinery.

The next advance in steam engine technology involved the realization that steam itself, rather than the condensing of steam to create a vacuum, could power an engine. The American inventor Oliver Evans designed the first high-pressure, non-condensing engine by 1804. Evans's engine, which was stationary (stood still), operated at 30 revolutions per minute (rpm) and was used to power a marble-cutting saw. The high-pressure engines used large cylindrical tanks of water, heated from beneath, to produce steam.

Piping System

*Scottish engineer
James Watt
contributed most to
the development of
the modern steam
engine.*

The first practical alternative to these large boilers was introduced by John Stevens, a pioneer of the American steamboat. This new boiling system used rows of long, narrow pipes to carry water through flames. Water recirculated until it was converted to high-pressure steam, which then forced itself out of the pipes. The Stevens boiler system, however, frequently exploded when its pressure grew too great for the boiler and pipes to contain.

In the 1860s and 1870s, George Corliss essentially perfected the steam engine. His large engines operated so smoothly that they could power textile (cloth) mills in Scotland without breaking delicate threads. Yet they were large enough to power all the exhibits at the Machinery Hall during Philadelphia's 1876 Centennial Exhibition.

Since the late nineteenth century, gasoline-powered engines have largely replaced steam engines in the industrial market. Even today, however, steam turbines (rotors) are used in the production of large quantities of energy for secondary distribution. In secondary distribution, the steam is used twice, once for energy and then for heat.

 # Stereo

"Stereo" is short for "stereophonic." *Stereo* is the Greek word for "three dimensional" and *phonic* means "sound." A stereo is a sound reproduction system in which two channels are used to give the illusion of a natural, fuller sound that reaches the listener from different directions.

Early Days

The first stereo had two groups of **microphones**, which were placed on either side of a stage. These microphones relayed the sound of a stage performance directly to two telephone receivers, which paying subscribers held to their ears. A German, Clement Ader, received a patent for the first stereophonic system on August 30, 1881. He displayed his invention the same year at the Paris Exposition in France.

During World War I (1914-18), a similar system was used to locate enemy **aircraft**. Two large horns were connected by rubber tubes to the ears of operators. Using these horns, the operators could hear from what direction enemy planes were coming.

In the 1930s, further progress was made in stereophonic systems. The Bell Telephone Laboratories developed a system in which electrical signals were sent through separate **amplifiers** to loudspeakers. Later, headphones improved on this system. When signals were fed to the left and right earpiece, a good stereo effect was produced.

British engineer Alan Dower Blumlein created the first stereo recording. The record contained two sets of information: the left-hand signal was engraved on the inside of the record's groove, while the right-hand signal appeared on the outside of the groove.

Newer Models

Since the 1970s, stereo has become far more sophisticated. **Magnetic recording** tapes and compact discs are among the foremost developments affecting stereo sound. Sound engineers created four-channel stereo (quadraphony), often called "surround" sound, which consists of four microphones, four amplifiers, and four loudspeakers that together provide remarkably realistic sound reproduction.

See also **Noise reduction system**

Storm

A storm is a disturbance of Earth's atmosphere with strong winds accompanied by rain or snow and sometimes thunder and lightning.

Types of Storms

The most common violent change in the weather is the thunderstorm. In the United States, thunderstorms usually occur in the late spring and summertime. Thunderstorms are rare in the parts of the country where the air tends to be colder, such as the New England states, North Dakota, and Montana. They are also rare by the Pacific Ocean, where summers are dry. The southeastern states tend to have the most thunderstorms.

Hurricanes are tropical storms that generate over warm ocean waters off West Africa and move westward toward Central America and the east-

Satellite map of Cyclone Forrest heading toward Bangladesh, November 20, 1992. Cyclones, hurricanes, and typhoons are powerful storms that follow the paths of tropical ocean currents.

What Causes Thunder and Lightning?

Two conditions must exist for a thunderstorm to occur. First, there must be rising currents of warm air called updrafts. Second, the updrafts must contain water vapor.

The rising air cools and condenses (changes to a liquid). The water vapor changes to either drops of water or ice that form a thundercloud. The air currents cause the water drops or ice crystals (hailstones) to collide, which produces electric charges. These charges can jump from cloud to cloud or from cloud to Earth. This movement is called lightning.

Lightning heats and rapidly expands the nearby air. Then the air cools and contracts. This expansion and contraction produces the vibrations that we hear as thunder.

If you count the number of seconds between seeing a flash of lightning and hearing the sound of thunder, then divide that number by 5, the answer will be the number of miles away that the lightning flashed.

The annual death toll from lightning is greater than the toll from hurricanes and tornadoes.

ern United States. The same type of storm in the western Pacific is referred to as a typhoon. Australians call them cyclones. In all cases, these powerful storms follow the paths of tropical ocean currents, increasing their size and strength until they reach land or more northern latitudes.

Tropical storms are classified as hurricanes when their winds reach 75 miles per hour (120 kph). In addition to high, sustained winds, hurricanes deliver heavy rain and devastating ocean waves. They can also produce tornadoes along their outer margins.

Monsoons are groups of storms that bring heavy rains to India, Southeast Asia, and Northern Australia for about three months, from June to September. Very hot, humid ocean winds blow landward at this time. During the remainder of the year, dry continental winds dominate. Unlike hurricanes, monsoons do not have high winds.

Tornadoes are violent windstorms that usually last only a short time. Tornadoes occur when twisting columns of air form beneath a thundercloud. Other types of storms include waterspouts, which are tornadoes over water. Dust devils are sudden updrafts of warm air that pick up dust and small objects in a swirling cyclical pattern and occur in hot, dry conditions.

Are Storms Good for Us?

Storms have good points and bad points. The precipitation (rain) from them is essential for agriculture and water supplies. Lightning is helpful in that it returns to Earth much of the negative electrical charge that leaks into the atmosphere. At the same time, storms can harm life and property. Some 150 Americans die from lightning strikes each year, and 250 more are injured.

See also **Atmospheric circulation; Weather forecasting model**

⋆⋆⋆ Subatomic particle

The technology of the late twentieth century has shown us that particles even smaller than atoms exist in our universe.

For nearly 100 years after John Dalton announced his **atomic theory** in 1803, it was widely accepted among scientists. His theory stated that all matter consists of tiny particles (atoms) that could not be divided.

Electrons, Protons, and Neutrons

However, the theory was profoundly shaken in the 1890s with Joseph John Thomson's discovery of the **electron**. It immediately became obvious that atoms consist of even smaller (called subatomic) particles. Electrons were one of them. Furthermore, the existence of the electron led to the belief that at least one other subatomic particle existed, because electrons are negatively charged and atoms are electrically neutral. Therefore, some positively charged subatomic particle must also exist. That particle, the **proton**, was discovered by Ernest Rutherford in 1919.

Strong evidence also existed for the presence of yet a third subatomic particle. This particle, the **neutron**, was discovered by James Chadwick in 1932.

A new atomic model that included only protons, neutrons, and electrons appealed to scientists because of its simplicity and because it explained most of the known physical phenomena. But in 1928, Paul Dirac predicted the existence of a paradox: a positively charged electron, the positron. Four years later, Carl David Anderson found Dirac's particle in a cosmic ray shower.

Dirac's theory suggested that *all* particles should have an antiparticle. The difference between the two would be a positive versus a negative charge. The search for the antiproton took until 1955. That year Owen

Chamberlain and Emilio Segré found the antiproton in the products of a nuclear reaction conducted at the University of California.

Hundreds of Subatomic Particles

The family of subatomic particles was soon to be expanded even more. Japanese physicist Hideki Yukawa developed the meson theory to explain the force of attraction that holds protons and neutrons together in the nucleus (the "strong" force). His calculations showed that such a force would be carried by a particle that lay between an electron and a proton.

At the very time that Yukawa was developing his meson theory, a technological breakthrough was taking place that was to revolutionize the

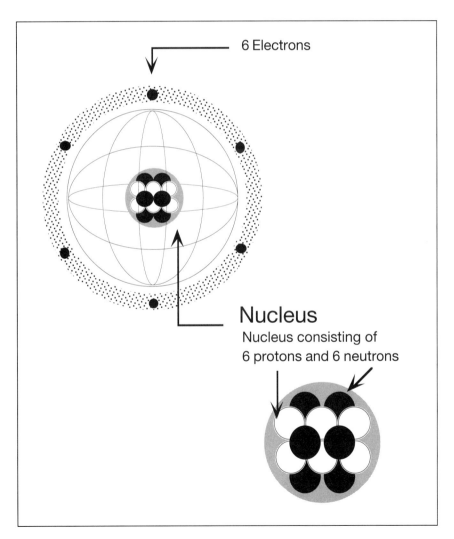

6 Electrons

Nucleus

Nucleus consisting of 6 protons and 6 neutrons

A carbon atom. Atoms consist of even smaller particles: electrons, protons, and neutrons.

study of subatomic particles. That breakthrough began with the invention of machines that can accelerate particles to very high energies. Experiments conducted with these machines soon revealed the existence of well over 100 new subatomic particles.

Grouping Particles

Before long, physicists were overwhelmed with the apparent chaos of the "particle zoo" that was being revealed to them. They turned their attention to bringing some organization to the "zoo."

Over the past two decades, physicists have refined their methods of classifying subatomic particles to produce what is now commonly known as the Standard Model. According to the Standard Model, two basic types of particles exist: quarks and leptons. Quarks and leptons are thought to be *fundamental* particles, in that they have no dimensions. They are similar to geometric points in space. Six kinds of each particle exist, arranged in pairs according to energy level.

See also **Particle accelerator**

⁎⁎ Submarine

A submarine is a ship capable of operating under water. Because its great advantage is its ability to stay hidden, it has developed as a tool of warfare.

In 1578 author William Bourne, in his book *Inventions or Devices,* described a ship with two hulls (bodies), one made of wood, the other of leather. According to Bourne, such a ship could be submerged or raised by taking in or expelling water from between the double hulls.

It is not known if the ship Bourne described was ever built, but a Dutch inventor, Cornelius Drebbel, did build a ship consisting of greased leather over a wooden framework. It was propelled either on or beneath the surface by eight oars sealed through the sides with leather flaps. During a demonstration for King James I of England in 1620, Drebbel's vessel was successfully piloted just under the surface of the Thames River in London. It could not make deep descents, however.

During the American Revolution (1776-81), American inventor David Bushnell built a one-man submarine called the *Turtle.* It was 6 feet (2 m) tall and resembled a squashed egg. It had two hand-cranked screw

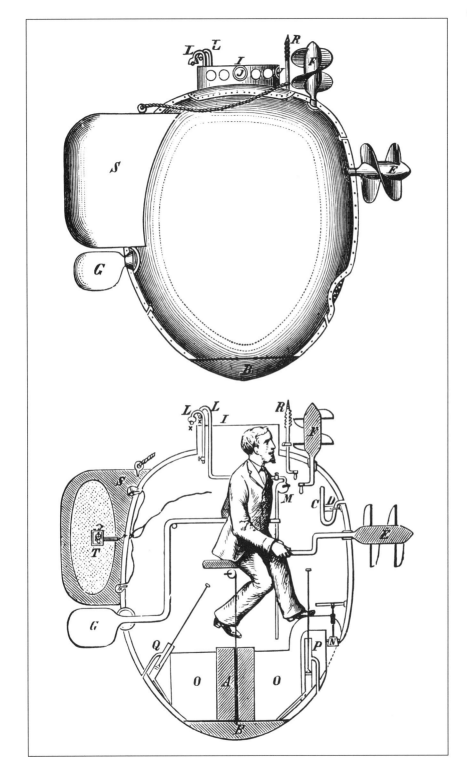

Nineteenth-century engraving of David Bushnell's submarine, the Turtle, which he designed during the Revolutionary War to carry and attach charges of gunpowder to the hulls of British ships.

propellers, a hand-operated control lever connected to the rudder, foot-operated pumps to let water in or send it out (to submerge or surface), and a control panel. The *Turtle* also had a large explosive attached to it so the operator could maneuver under an enemy ship, screw the explosive into the ship's hull, and depart before the explosive's timing device discharged it. On its one and only test mission, the *Turtle* failed to sink its target.

Robert Fulton

Perhaps the most successful early submarine was designed by American inventor Robert Fulton. Fulton lived in an age of naval battles but hated war. He hoped that a device that could make warships ineffective would end war altogether. In 1801 he built a 21-foot (6 m) vessel with a two-bladed propeller, which he called *Nautilus.*

Fulton, who was living in France at the time, tried to interest both the French and the British governments in his idea. These major naval powers did not want to participate in developing a weapon that could compromise their military strength. Fulton abandoned the submarine project, returned home, and went on to produce his famous steamboats in the United States.

After the American Civil War (1861-65), designers sought alternatives to human-powered propulsion for submarines. The self-propelled **torpedo** was invented in 1866. Several systems proved unsuitable—**steam engines** made the craft unbearably hot and an electric **battery** could not be recharged at sea.

In the late 1890s, Irish-born American John Holland solved these problems by adding a second power source, the gasoline engine, to the batteries then in use. Because it needed oxygen, the gasoline engine could not be used while a submarine was underwater. When the ship was above water, its engine could provide propulsion to move the ship forward and could charge the batteries used while the ship was submerged. Holland's vessels incorporated many of the features in modern submarines: a powerful engine, advanced control and balancing systems, and a circular-shaped hull to withstand pressure. The U.S. Navy accepted his submarine, the U.S.S. *Holland,* in 1900.

Periscopes and Diesel Engines

Around this time, two other improvements were introduced. Inventor Simon Lake created the first periscope specifically for submarines. A periscope is a vertical telescope that provides a magnified view and a wide angle of vision. In the 1890s, Rudolf Diesel invented an engine that was

fired by compression rather than an electric spark. The diesel engine was more economical than the gasoline engine and its fumes were much less toxic (poisonous) and volatile (unpredictable). This new engine became essential to all submarines until nuclear power was introduced as a means of propulsion in the 1950s.

In World War II (1939-45), submarines played a large role in Germany's repeated attacks on Allied (English, United States, and French) ships. Meanwhile, American submarines crippled the Japanese by sinking nearly 1,400 merchant and naval ships. During this time, the snorkel was developed. It was a set of two fixed air pipes that projected from the sub's topside. One tube brought fresh air into the vessel, and the other vented engine exhaust fumes. Now a sub could stay hidden below the surface when running on its diesel engine and recharging its batteries.

Nuclear Power

The greatest modern advance in submarine technology was the introduction of nuclear power. With the encouragement of U.S. Navy captain Hyman Rickover, American inventors designed the U.S.S. *Nautilus,* the first nuclear-powered submarine. Launched in 1955, the U.S.S. *Nautilus* carried a reactor in which controlled **nuclear fission** provided the heat that converted water into steam for turbines. With this new power source, the submarine could remain under water indefinitely and cruise at top speed for any length of time required.

The traditional needle-like shape proved inefficient for such a submarine. A new teardrop design was introduced in the United States. Vessels with this improved shape easily drove through the water at speeds of 35 to 40 knots per hour (about 40.25 to 46 mph). The U.S. Navy later adopted this shape for its submarines.

⋆⋆ Subway

Mass transit systems have been developed to relieve one of the horrors of modern city life: the rush hour traffic jam. Mass transit systems combine different types of transportation, such as ground-level and above-ground **train** and bus lines to take large numbers of passengers to their destinations. A good mass transit system almost eliminates the need for individual cars.

In many cities, subways are a part of the mass transit system. They are underground rail lines that offer a relatively speedy ride to and from the city center.

Subways are usually built in alignment with existing streets, because the below-ground-level part of office buildings obstructs any alternative. Beyond the city center, the trains may go in any direction and may run beneath rivers and harbors. Some subways, such as Montreal's Metro, run several levels below the city center. Its upper levels are used for shops, offices, museums, and hotels. Construction costs, which can be millions of dollars per mile, make subways impractical in areas where they will not be heavily used.

Early Subways

The first subway, suggested by city lawyer Charles Pearson, opened in London in 1863. In the first year, it carried 9,500,000 passengers on steam locomotives that burned coke and coal, both major pollutants. In 1866 work began on what is now known as The Tube after tunneling methods were perfected. Electricity was in use by 1890, and all subways built

The New York subway system was begun in 1904 and is now the largest system in the world.

Open-Cut and Tubular Subways

Two types of rail subways exist, the open-cut and the tubular. The open-cut subway is constructed by digging a trench, then covering it after a **tunnel** structure has been put into place. Open-cut subways are rectangular in shape.

The tubular subway, also known as the tube, is constructed by boring a long round hole parallel to the ground surface. The surface is broken up only for passenger stations and ventilation shafts.

since then have used electric trains, which are quieter and do not fill the subway passages with pollution.

In 1896 Budapest, Hungary, became the first city in continental Europe to open a subway. The Paris Metro opened four years later. Boston, Massachusetts, opened the first subway in the United States in 1897. The New York subway system was begun in 1904 and is now the largest system in the world.

Dozens of other subway systems have been built in cities worldwide. San Francisco's Bay Area Rapid Transit System (BART), built in 1971, was the first fully automated subway system, eliminating the use of human drivers. In many cities in the United States, the movement of major employers to the suburbs has posed a new challenge to mass transportation planners, who find themselves with more routes to cover and fewer passengers per route.

See also **Tunnel**

★ Sulfonamide drug

Sulfa drugs are eaten or injected.

The sulfonamides, also known as sulfa drugs, halt the growth of **bacteria**. Their discovery paved the way for cheap and effective treatment of frequently fatal bacterial infections such as pneumonia.

Before 1932 no synthetic (man-made) chemicals existed for the treatment of bacterial infections. A new era was ushered in by the German chemist Gerhard Domagk when he began a search for chemical substances to kill bacteria within the human body.

Domagk served as director of the Laboratory for Experimental Pathology and Bacteriology at I. G. Farbenindustrie, a German dye company. There he tested the properties of dyes synthesized by his colleagues for their use as drugs. Certain dyes—those containing a sulfonamide group—seemed to bind tightly to wool fabrics, indicating an attraction to protein molecules. Because bacteria are protein, Domagk reasoned that these dyes might fasten to bacteria, inhibiting or killing them. In 1932 he discovered that a dye called Prontosil controlled streptococcal infections in mice and staphylococcal infections in rabbits with no damage to the animals.

Domagk's employer began tests of the effects of Prontosil on infections in humans. Domagk had an unexpected opportunity to test the dye's effectiveness close to home, when a needle-prick in his lab accidentally infected his young daughter with streptococcus (strep). Uncertain of what the outcome would be, he gave her Prontosil. She made a rapid recovery. It was clear that Prontosil had the ability to control streptococcus infections in humans. Prontosil was given in 1936 to the son of U.S. president Franklin Roosevelt. Franklin D. Roosevelt, Jr., thought to be dying, recovered from a streptococcal infection.

In 1936 French chemists and husband and wife Jacques Trefouel and Thérèse Trefouel, working with Daniele Bovet, separated sulfanilamide, the parent sulfa compound, from Prontosil. They found that sulfanilamide, and not the dye itself, kills bacteria. Since then, more than 5,000 sulfa drugs have been prepared and tested. Because repeated exposure to the sulfa drugs caused bacteria to become resistant to most of them, fewer than 20 sulfa drugs have been found to continue to kill the same bacteria strains.

The introduction of **antibiotics** such as **penicillin** has decreased the need for sulfa drugs. However, they are still useful in the treatment of streptococcal infections, urinary tract infections, and ulcerative colitis. In addition, sulfanilamide is still used in veterinary medicine.

✦ Sun

The Sun is actually a star. We are closer to it than to any other star. To people in ancient times, the Sun was a god. They believed that the Sun revolved around Earth.

The Sun ia a ball of glowing gases.

What Early Astronomers Thought

The idea that the sun revolved around Earth lasted until the sixteenth century, when Polish astronomer Nicolaus Copernicus demonstrated that the Sun is actually at the center of the universe. Italian philosopher Giordano Bruno (1548-1600) thought the universe was infinite (lasting forever), with a countless number of suns in it.

Around 1610, **Galileo Galilei** studied the Sun with a new instrument, the **telescope.** He noted spots that shifted position from day to day. He used this information to determine the Sun's rotation rate. Fifty years later, **Isaac Newton** passed sunlight through a prism and saw that it was composed of all the colors of the spectrum. So began the science of **spectroscopy**, based on the principle of separation of light according to its frequencies, or wavelengths.

The Ancients believed that the Sun revolved around Earth until the sixteenth century, when Polish astronomer Nicolaus Copernicus proved otherwise.

One hundred fifty years later, British physicist William Hyde Wollaston discovered dark lines in the spectrum where light was missing. German physicist Joseph von Fraunhofer counted 600 such lines. These lines were a mystery until 1859, when another German physicist, Gustav Kirchhoff, explained that the dark lines were caused by elements in the Sun. These elements absorb the wavelengths of light. If observers knew which elements corresponded to those wavelengths, they would know what the Sun was made of. This became possible in 1864, when the first elements were identified. (Today more than 60 elements have been identified in the solar spectrum.)

How the Sun Produces Energy

How the Sun produces its energy remained a mystery until 1938, when German-born American physicist Hans Bethe worked out the details of **nuclear fusion.** Deep in the Sun's core, where the temperature is in the millions of degrees Celsius, nuclear fusion takes place. Four atoms of hydrogen fuse into two atoms of helium. The two helium atoms contain slightly less mass than the original four hydrogen atoms because some mass has been converted into energy.

What We Now Know About the Sun

The Sun is a ball of incandescent (glowing) gases. About 75 percent of the Sun is **hydrogen**.

The Sun Is Born

The Sun is believed to have formed from a great nebula (a cloud of dust and gas) 4.5 billion years ago. The "nebular hypothesis" was first proposed by German philosopher Immanuel Kant (1724-1804) and, independently, by French astronomer Pierre Laplace (1749-1827). The cloud collapsed under its own gravity, producing heat. The heat caused nuclear fusion.

The Sun then began to shine. Scientists believe the Sun will shine for another five billion years or more. When nuclear fusion ceases in the core, the Sun will expand and become a red giant star, engulfing Earth. The outer solar shell could puff off, forming a planetary nebula. Left behind will be a small, dense white dwarf star.

Knowledge about our Sun provides insight into the nature of other types of stars as well, from the hot blue-white giants to the cool red dwarfs.

Warning: Never look directly at the Sun. You may suffer permanent eye damage.

Helium makes up about 23 percent. The remaining 2 percent includes **carbon**, **nitrogen**, **oxygen**, and **neon**, among others.

Sunspots are not actual "spots" on the Sun's surface. They are regions that are 2735° F (1500° C) cooler than the surrounding area—the contrast makes them look black by comparison—and are magnetic storms.

The Sun's glowing, white-hot surface is called the photosphere. Above the photosphere is a glowing red layer of hydrogen gas called the chromosphere. A pale ring of gases called the corona extends millions of miles above the chromosphere. The **solar wind**, a stream of electrically charged particles, blows from the corona. Heat, light, and radio waves originate in the corona of the Sun.

Solar Activities

Prominences are clouds of flaming gas that look like flames rising above the Sun. Some prominences that rise from the Sun's surface can be almost 40,000 miles high and last for several days.

Solar flares are explosions on the Sun's surface that occur mainly during periods of sunspot activity. They produce an incredible amount of energy in only five to ten minutes. The largest flares generate enough energy to supply the United States's needs for 100,000 years. Flares are primarily responsible for producing the aurora borealis (northern lights) and the aurora australis (southern lights) in Earth's atmosphere.

⋆⋆ Supercomputer

Supercomputers are the most powerful computers that exist at a given time. They can do complicated calculations quickly and (usually) sell for the highest price.

The Cray 1 Computer, designed by Seymour Cray, founder of Cray Computer Corporation of Colorado Springs, Colorado, is generally regarded as the first supercomputer. Cray, who had previously worked for UNIVAC and later helped found Control Data Corporation and Cray Research, Inc., made his lifelong goal the production of the world's most powerful computers. Until the late 1980s, Cray fulfilled that goal nearly all of the time, but with increasing competition from other U.S. and Japanese designers.

*Seymour Cray poses
with the liquid
immersion
technology for the
Cray 2 Computer in
1983.*

Uses

Supercomputers are used for tasks such as oil and mineral prospecting, analysis of subatomic activity, and studying Earth's changing ozone layer. Computer design projects include design of **aircraft**, microprocessors, anti-missile deflection systems, and ships. Supercomputers are also used for simulation (re-creation or modeling) of weather systems, the birth of the universe, nuclear reactions, and **DNA (deoxyribonucleic acid)**.

See also **Computer operating system; Microcomputer; Minicomputer**

⋆⋆⋆ Superconductivity

Dutch physicist Heike Kamerlingh Onnes discovered superconductivity in 1911. Superconductivity is a condition occurring in many metals and alloys (combinations of metals), usually at low temperatures. In superconductivity, an electric current will persist indefinitely without any voltage. Kamerlingh Onnes called the temperature at which a metal becomes superconducting the metal's "transition temperature." He also noted that external **magnetic fields** applied to a metal could eliminate superconductivity in a metal, even below its transition temperature.

The property of superconductivity has some obvious practical applications. In most electrical devices, a large fraction of the energy that flows into the device is wasted in overcoming resistance within the device. If the device could be made with superconducting materials, its efficiency could be greatly improved, often by 50 percent or more.

In super-conductivity, an electric current will persist indefinitely without any voltage.

Studies in Superconductivity

The most significant breakthrough in superconductivity theory occurred with the announcement of the BCS theory in 1957. The acronym "BCS" stands for the names of the three scientists who developed the theory, John Bardeen, Leon Cooper, and J. Robert Schrieffer.

According to the BCS theory, an electron moving through a crystal lattice (grid) tends to distort the lattice. This distortion creates a wave of positive charge resulting from the dislocation of positive ions in the lattice. This positive charge attracts to it a second electron which, with the first electron, forms a Cooper pair that sweeps through the crystal. The accu-

Superconducting Super Collider

One of the first applications planned for superconductivity was the Superconducting Super Collider (SSC). The SSC was intended to be the world's most powerful **particle accelerator**. The most important factor holding back its construction was the cost of its magnets. With the availability of new superconducting materials, the potential cost of building the SSC dropped considerably. However, the project was still considered too expensive and was canceled in 1994.

mulation of Cooper pairs, all flowing in the same direction, results in the resistantless flow characteristic of a superconductor.

The work of the BCS team had little impact on the discovery of new superconducting materials. Then, in 1986, a startling breakthrough occurred. Two physicists working at the IBM Research Laboratories in Zurich—K. Alex Müller and Georg Bednorz—announced the discovery of a new type of ceramic substance that becomes superconductive at 35° K.

In little more than a year, other researchers around the world produced similar ceramics. Transition temperatures for these materials shot up from 35° K to 40° K to 52° K to nearly 100° K. At long last, there seemed to be some possibility of making superconducting electrical devices that can operate at near-room temperatures. Still, very little progress has since been made in the commercial application of these results.

⋆⋆ Surfboard

Hundreds of years ago, the Polynesians who lived on the scattered group of islands in the Pacific Ocean near Australia were the first to ride ocean waves on surfboards. They used two types of boards: the *alaia* and the *olo*.

The smaller alaia boards weighed only about 11 pounds (4.98 kg) and were made from the breadfruit tree. They were ridden by women and children. The larger olo boards weighed 160 pounds (72.43 kg) and were carved with tools made of stone or bone and then smoothed and polished by hand.

Surfboards were made this way until early in the twentieth century. Duke Paoa Kahanamoku, a Hawaiian Olympic champion swimmer, was among those who worked on improving surfboard construction and design. Inventor Tom Blake built the first paddleboard—a big, hollow board with straight rails (sides), a semi-pointed tail, and laminated wood for the deck (top surface). Laminated wood is composed of many layers of wood pressed together.

After World War II (1939-45), surfboard builders in Hawaii and California came up with many innovations. Single and double skegs (fins) were tried, along with various changes in shape. Boards during this period were made of solid wood, laminated wood, or **plastic.** The introduction of foam **rubber** and fiberglass made wood obsolete (out of date) as a primary material. Other design improvements included the creation of scoop noses that allowed the tips of surfboards to stay on the surface rather than dip under the waves.

Scoop noses allow the tips of surfboards to stay on the surface rather than dip under the waves.

The largest version of the Swiss army knife weighs about 7 ounces and has 29 attachments, including a ballpoint pen, a magnifying glass, and a leather-stitching needle.

⋆⋆ Swiss army knife

The Swiss army knife was first produced in Switzerland for the military by Karl Elsener in 1891. It was a wood-handled device that contained a number of useful tools in addition to the standard knife blade. By pressing a spring mechanism, the knife owner could access utensils such as a bottle opener, screwdriver, or fingernail file. These utensils folded up alongside the blade. Elsener also designed a knife for civilian use. That one had a red handle so that it could be found easily in snow.

Today, the Victorinox Cutlery Corporation, whose president is the inventor's great-grandson, continues to make the Swiss army knife. The largest version, called the Swiss Champ, weighs about 7 ounces and has 29 attachments, including a ballpoint pen, a magnifying glass, and a leather-stitching needle.

⋆⋆ Synapse

"Synapse" comes from the Greek words for "point of contact" and "join together." Synapse is the place in a nerve **cell** where nerve impulses ("messages") pass through.

Makeup of Nerve Cells

Nerve cells contain very long projections called nerve fibers. In humans and animals, nerve fibers overlap each other in a very complicated network. For this reason, early biologists had trouble seeing exactly what made up a single nerve cell and how two nerve cells are related to each other.

In the late 1800s, German anatomist Wilhelm von Waldeyer-Hartz suggested that two nerve cells or nerve fibers are not actually in contact with each other, but are separated by a small gap. Waldeyer-Hartz's hypothesis was confirmed in the laboratory by Italian histologist Camillo Golgi. A histologist studies plant and animal **tissues**. However, Golgi could

Synapses between nerve cells in a rabbit's brain. Nerve messages travel along one cell, jump the gap (synapse) between two cells, then land on the second cell.

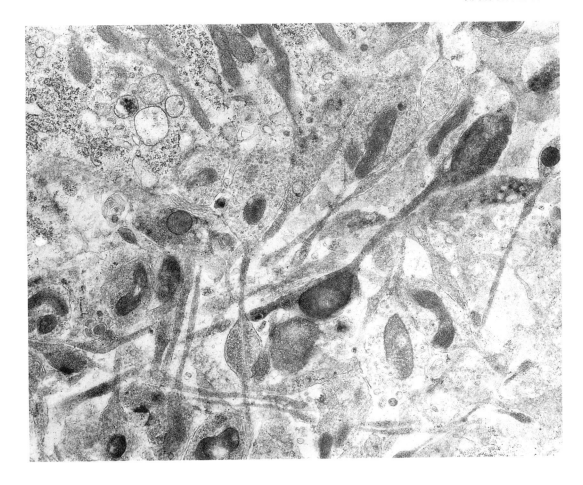

not explain how this gap was involved in sending nerve impulses from one cell to another.

British physiologist Charles Scott Sherrington presented a clear description of nerve transmission in 1906. In his book *The Integrative Action of the Nervous System*, Sherrington stated that nerve messages travel along one cell, jump the gap between two cells, and land on the second cell. He was unable to say, however, how the message passes across the gap, which he called the "synapse."

Sherrington's description inspired efforts by other researchers to learn how nerve messages pass across the synapse. Another British physiologist, Thomas R. Elliott, suggested in 1903 that these messages might be carried across the synapse by chemicals. Over the next two decades, research confirmed this hypothesis and uncovered the first of these chemicals, **acetylcholine**.

✦ Synthesizer, music

A synthesizer can control and change the beginning of a sound, its duration, and its fading, in addition to controlling the waveform itself.

The synthesizer is a device that creates sounds electronically and allows the user to change and manipulate the sounds. All sounds in nature are made by waves of varying air pressure. A synthesizer creates sounds by generating an electrical signal in the form of a waveform, usually either a sine wave or other simple mathematical wave, which is amplified and used to drive an acoustic speaker.

Unfortunately, the sound quality of a simple waveform is somewhat "raw" and unmusical, at least to most people. The waveform is usually altered in numerous ways, using filters to create the interesting timbres, or colors, of sound that are usually associated with certain acoustical instruments. Changing the frequency of the waveform raises or lowers the pitch of the sound. A synthesizer can control and change the beginning of a sound, its duration, and its fading, in addition to controlling the waveform itself.

Synthesizers can receive information from numerous sources about how to set the different parameters of its output sound. An electronic device, such as a computer program, or a person can control the synthesizer. An obvious way to accomplish this is to build the synthesizer to resemble an already existing musical instrument, such as a piano. A piano-like keyboard is often used to generate signals that control the pitch of the synthesizer, although a keyboard is not required, or even necessarily desirable, to do the job. One of the first commercially available keyboard-based synthesizers marketed to the general public was built by Robert Moog in the 1960s.

All of the early synthesizers were built using analog computer technology, which operates with numbers reresented by measurable quantities, like voltages. Since the late 1970s, however, digital synthesis has developed as the preferred technology in synthesizer design. In the process of digitally recording a sound, called sampling, any sound recording can be converted into a series of numbers that a computer can analyze. The computer takes "snapshots" of the sampled sound in very short increments, about 40,000 times a second. Mathematical techniques are then used to calculate the complex waveform of the original sound. The sound can then be easily reproduced in real-time from a synthesizer keyboard.

This and other techniques for creating sounds form the design basis of most digital synthesizers such as the New England Digital Synclavier and the Kurzweil music synthesizer. The same technique can be applied to synthesize drums, voices or any other kind of sound. Digital instruments can also receive input not just from a keyboard, but from the actual breath of the performer, for instance. Digital flutes and other wind-instrument synthesizers convert the force of the musician's breath into a signal that can modify any desired feature of the output sound.

Synthesizers have shown themselves capable of creating a wide variety of new and interesting sounds. Their one limitation, of course, is that they sound only as good as the speaker that amplifies their signal. Most humans can hear sounds far beyond the range that even the best speakers can reproduce, sounds that acoustical instruments have always been capable of generating. Because of this limitation (and others), synthesizers are not viewed as replacements of traditional instruments, but rather as creative tools that enhance musical possibilities.

The process of digitally recording a sound is called "sampling."

⋆⋆⋆ Syphilis

Syphilis is a serious disease transmitted through sexual activity. Although modern treatments now control the disease, the number of people suffering from syphilis remains high. It is a public health concern around the world.

Three Stages

Syphilis can be cured through doses of penicillin. However, many people remain untreated, either through ignorance or because they mistakenly believe that syphilis cannot harm them. Untreated syphilis has three stages.

In the first stage, between one and eight weeks after infection occurs, a small, hard, painless swelling, called a primary (or Hunter's) chancre (pronounced "shanker") appears. The sore usually heals in one to five weeks. However, during that period, disease bacteria circulate throughout the body via the bloodstream.

The second stage appears about six weeks after the sore disappears. Symptoms include a general feeling of being ill, fever, headache, and a loss of appetite. Glands may swell in the groin or neck, and a skin rash may develop. This second stage can last two to six weeks.

Some historians suggest that Queen Elizabeth I of England was left unable to bear children because of a syphilis infection.

The third stage, called latent or late syphilis, can last for years. No symptoms are present, and only a special blood test shows the presence of the disease. During this stage, the disease will finally flare up without warning, affecting the brain and heart. At this point, the disease is no longer treatable. Symptoms of third stage syphilis include blindness, sterility, and insanity.

Syphilis in History

Spanish physician Rodrigo Ruiz de Isla wrote of treating syphilis patients in Barcelona in 1493. He claimed that the soldiers of explorer Christopher Columbus contracted the disease in the Caribbean and brought it back to Europe in 1492. However, others challenge this statement. Some medical historians believe that syphilis has been present from ancient times but was either mislabeled or misdiagnosed.

Italian physician and writer Girolamo Fracastoro gave the disease its name in his poem "Syphilis sive morbus Gallicus" ("Syphilis, or the French Disease"), published in 1530. However, for centuries after that, the disease was called "pox" or the "great pox." At that time, the treatment was **mercury**, used in vapor baths, as

Syphilis Versus Gonorrhea

A milder form of syphilis was long confused with **gonorrhea**. Then, in 1767, physician John Hunter, wishing to prove that syphilis and gonorrhea were two different diseases, infected himself with fluid from a patient who had gonorrhea. Unfortunately, Hunter did not know that the patient also had syphilis, and he developed the sore that is the first sign of syphilis (the sore that now bears his name).

The distinction between the two diseases was made clear in 1879, when German bacteriologist Albert Neisser isolated the bacterium responsible for gonorrhea.

an ointment, or taken orally. The mercury was supposed to increase the flow of saliva and phlegm to wash out the poisons. Unfortunately, mercury is a poison itself. Its side effects included loss of hair and teeth, abdominal pains, and mouth sores. Syphilis sufferers were not cured and often became more ill after taking mercury.

Testing for Syphilis

In 1905 German zoologist Fritz Schaudinn and his assistant Erich Hoffmann discovered the bacterium responsible for syphilis, the spiral-shaped *Treponema pallidum*. The following year, German physician August von Wassermann developed the first test to diagnose syphilis. The test involved checking for the syphilis **antibody** in a sample of **blood**. One drawback was that the test would take two days to complete.

Russian-American researcher Reuben Leon Kahn developed a modified test for syphilis in 1923. This test took only a few minutes to complete. Another test was developed by researchers William A. Hinton and J. A. V. Davies. Today fluorescent antibody tests are used for detection. Although there is yet no **inoculation** for syphilis, the disease can be controlled through education, safe sexual practices, and proper medical treatment.

Finding a Cure

In 1904 German research physician Paul Ehrlich began looking for a safe, effective treatment for syphilis. Working with Japanese bacteriologist Sahachiro Hata, he tested hundreds of derivatives of the arsenic-based compound atoxyl and finally found one that worked. Ehrlich called it "Salvarsan." Following trials of the substance on humans, Ehrlich and Hata

German research physician Paul Ehrlich found a safe, effective treatment for syphilis.

announced in 1911 that the drug was an effective cure for syphilis. The drug attacked the disease germs but did not harm healthy **cells**.

Ehrlich's work in the emerging field of **chemotherapy** (the use of chemical substances to treat diseases) earned him a Nobel Prize in 1908. He went on to develop two safer forms of the drug, including neosalvarsan in 1912 and sodium salvarsan in 1913.

Penicillin came into widespread use in treating bacterial diseases during World War II (1939-45). It was first used to against syphilis in 1943 by New York physician John F. Mahoney, and it remains the treatment of choice today. Other **antibiotics** are also effective.

See also **Fluorescence and phosphorescence**

⋆⋆ Teaching aid

A History

One of the earliest known teaching aids is the hornbook, which was used in English schools from the mid-fifteenth century (and later in colonial America) through the early nineteenth century. It was a flat board on which a sheet of paper printed with the alphabet, the Lord's prayer, and several simple words was pasted.

The blackboard probably evolved from the hornbook, and has become one of the most widely used teaching aids. It was patented in 1823 by Samuel Read Hall of Concord, Vermont, a Congregational minister who founded the Concord Academy to train teachers in "school keeping." Hall's version was made of pine board, made smooth by use of a carpenter's plane and painted black. Today, the blackboard is often called a chalkboard. It may be green instead of black and made of slate, glass, or wood.

The globe is another highly popular teaching aid. It provides a representation of the earth, and sometimes celestial (heavenly) bodies, that is true to scale, without the distortions of flat maps.

Globes are hollow spheres usually made of plastic or metal, and sometimes are translucent (see through) or inflatable. A map, cut in triangular or tapering strips called gores, is pasted or printed on the globe. A physical globe shows the natural characteristics (mountains, etc.), while a political globe shows countries, cities, etc. The globe can be mounted on an axis (usually tilted 23.5 degrees to simulate the angle of the earth's orbit around the Sun) or placed in a cradle.

Teaching aid

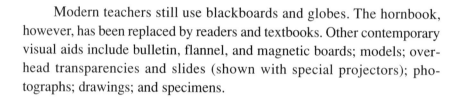

Globes Through History

The ancient Greeks realized that the earth was spherical and are known to have used globes as early as 150 B.C. The oldest existing celestial globe (showing the constellations) is the Farnese globe, made in A.D. 25. Another historic globe was made in 1492 by Martin Behaim of Nuremburg, Germany, who is thought to have influenced Christopher Columbus's decision to try to reach Asia by sailing west. In 1810 a Vermont farmer and copper engraver named James Wilson made the first American globes. He drew highly accurate maps that fit perfectly on wooden spheres. Many of his globe-making techniques are still used.

Modern teachers still use blackboards and globes. The hornbook, however, has been replaced by readers and textbooks. Other contemporary visual aids include bulletin, flannel, and magnetic boards; models; overhead transparencies and slides (shown with special projectors); photographs; drawings; and specimens.

The globe provides a representation of the earth that is true to scale.

Audio and Visual Aids

Audio aids include tape recordings (used, for instance, to teach foreign languages) and **radio**. Some students have established their own radio stations. Others are taught over the airwaves.

Audio-visual materials, especially **motion pictures**, include a broad category of teaching aids. During World War II (1939-45), educators saw their effectiveness in training large numbers of troops quickly. Films came into widespread classroom use in the 1940s and 1950s.

Students today can watch lectures on closed-circuit **television** (lectures transmitted to a limited number of reception stations). They can also view instructional videotapes and videodiscs.

When audio-visual materials are presented in an interactive format, they become part of a class of instructional media called teaching machines. These allow students to teach themselves, usually as they progress through a series of increasingly difficult questions. Using a teaching machine can be as simple as pressing a button to choose an answer, or as complex as "piloting" a flight simulator. The first such device was invented by Sydney L. Pressey in the 1920s. It tested students' knowledge by requiring them to press the correct levers before they could proceed to another question or problem.

Computers

Computers are the newest teaching machines. They can give students drills and practice lessons, tutorial help, and even carry on a limited "conversation." Some encyclopedias and references on CD-ROM are often multimedia. They contain audio and video clips that allow students to hear and see in action the subjects they are studying in addition to reading about them.

While some say computer-assisted instruction (CAI) is dehumanizing because it deprives students of vital personal contact, others claim that it frees teachers to spend more time working with individuals. Many agree that all students need to develop computer literacy as they prepare for the future.

A student learns about fractals using a computer. Computers are the newest teaching machines.

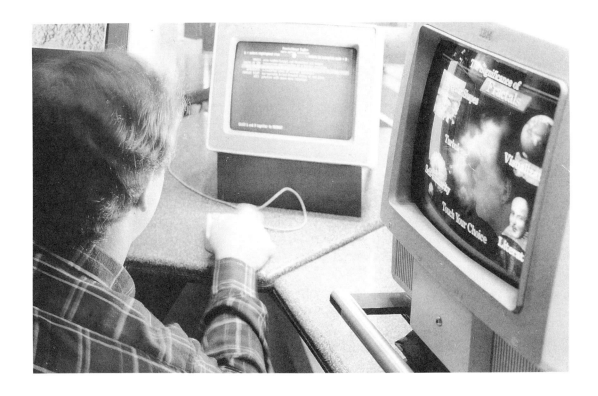

⋆⋆ Technetium

Technetium was the first element to be produced artifically.

The existence of element 43 was predicted as early as 1914, when British physicist Henry Moseley restructured the periodic table of the elements based on atomic numbers rather than atomic weights. It was clear to him that there should be two elements beneath **manganese** in the table. Researchers agreed and began looking for these elements.

It was known that a radioactive metallic element was produced during **nuclear fission** (a nuclear reaction during which the nucleus splits almost equally). This element was isolated and extracted in 1937 by Italian-born American physicist Emilio Segrè and C. Perrier, working at the University of Palermo in Italy. This substance, element 43, was the first element to be produced artificially. Segrè and Perrier suggested the name "technetium," from the Greek *technetos,* for "artificial."

Technetium is used in medicine. When technetium compounds (mixtures) are ingested (swallowed), they tend to concentrate in the liver and so are valuable in examining that organ. Technetium is also useful in the exploration of diseases of the circulatory system.

See also **Atomic and molecular weights; Periodic law; Radioactive tracer**

⋆⋆ Telephone answering device

Early Devices

The telephone answering machine was introduced by American manufacturer Code-A-Phone in 1958. Those early machines were large, clumsy, expensive devices that were used mostly by small businesses. They consisted of two separate tape players housed in a single cabinet. One played the outgoing message on a continuous-loop cartridge or cassette. The other was usually a reel-to-reel tape that recorded the incoming message. The telephone company required these machines to be connected to the telephone line through a coupler, owned and installed by them. Installation costs ranged from $10 to $50, and the customer also had to pay a monthly rental fee ranging from $3 to $8 for the coupler.

During the mid-1980s, demand for telephone answering machines took off. This was largely due to the increase in single-person households and households with more than one wage earner—people who left phones untended for long periods of time. Dramatic price drops also fueled their new-found popularity. Costs fell from over $750 to $100 and less, thanks mostly to cheaper production methods in the Far East. During 1985, sales rose 40 percent and machines were in short supply.

Modern Developments

The new generation of answering machines emphasized a machine that was much smaller, using just two small cassettes. Owners now could install the machines themselves without the telephone company's coupler.

Today's machines offer many features that were unknown in 1958. One can retrieve messages even when away from home by entering a personal code into a touch-tone phone and receiving a playback of recorded messages. Some machines allow you to change the outgoing message over the remote phone. Others announce the time and date of each message with an artificially generated voice. Some manufacturers now use an electronic chip in place of the outgoing message tape. Since the chip has no moving parts, it seldom breaks down.

PhoneMate's ADAM, available since 1990, is an All-Digital Answering Machine, the first phone answering device to use digital signal processing, which converts incoming messages into signals that are stored in memory rather than on tape.

Voice Mail

Voice mail is an alternative to answering machines. Used in offices since the early 1980s, it became available for home use through telephone companies in 1988. With voice mail, the phone itself becomes an electronic mailbox. Callers, directed by a voice, may leave a message for a specific family member or business associate. Each individual can retrieve his or her own messages by entering a personal code.

⋆ Telephone cable, transatlantic

Transatlantic (across the Atlantic Ocean) telephone communication over **radio** became possible in 1927. However, weather conditions frequently disrupted radio transmissions. An undersea cable seemed to be the logical answer to this problem, but this did not become possible until years later.

The plan was to lay the cable on top of the sea floor. This idea presented several difficult problems. It required using undersea repeaters, which boost a signal as it becomes weaker over distance. However, experience in other places showed that these repeaters often failed and were expensive to replace. Also, the interaction of wire and water caused distortion of the signals, and the materials needed to insulate the wires did not exist at the time.

Bell Labs, a high-tech research lab, tackled the repeater problem in the late 1940s, developing a repeater that would last for 20 years. At the same time, **plastic polyethylene** was developed and proved to have excellent insulating properties. A test line was laid between Miami, Florida, and Havana, Cuba, in 1950. It was successful enough for American Telephone & Telegraph (AT&T), the telephone giant, to plan a transatlantic cable.

In June 1955 the ship *Monarch* set out from Newfoundland, Canada, laying cable and adding a repeater every 10 to 40 miles. The *Monarch* reached Scotland in September. The following summer the ship made a return cable-laying voyage. The resulting transatlantic telephone line went into service in September 1956.

Beginning in 1988, fiber optic transatlantic cables solved the problems posed by wire and satellite transmissions, such as distortion and electromagnetic interference.

Each cable could handle many different telephone conversations. On the first full day of service, 75 percent more cross-Atlantic telephone calls were made by cable than had been made by radio in the previous ten days. The world community responded enthusiastically to the reality of live person-to-person communication across the ocean. Overseas lines were laid at a steady rate.

Satellite transmission of telephone communications challenged underwater cables beginning in 1962. Satellite signals, however, were often hindered by electromagnetic interference, which blocked high-speed transmission of data. Since telephone use increasingly involved data (computers, faxes, etc.) as opposed to voice messages, this interference became more troublesome. Also, satellite transmissions could be easily intercepted.

Beginning in 1988, fiber optic transatlantic cables solved these problems, offering very secure transmissions with little interference. In fiber optics, microscopically tiny glass cables carry pulses of light encoded with telephone and data messages.

⁺⋆⁺ Teleprinter and teletype

The teleprinter is a typewriter-printer that sends messages over telegraph or other data communication lines to a receiving printer, which automatically prints the message. The teleprinter is also called a teletypewriter. The person who is sending the message types it on a typewriter-like keyboard. The keyboard converts each keystroke to a coded electrical impulse and sends it to the receiver printer, which decodes the impulses to reproduce the original keystrokes.

The teleprinter was first developed by Frederick G. Creed, a Canadian who was inspired by his work as a telegrapher to find a way to send printed messages without using Morse code. Creed immigrated to Scotland in 1897, where he modified a typewriter he invented to produce the first teleprinter. The British Post Office bought a dozen of Creed's machines in 1902, but their use did not catch on at first.

In the United States, Charles L. Krumm designed the prototype (first version) of the modern teleprinter in 1907. A refined version of this machine was widely marketed in the United States in the 1920s. It was most often referred to by its American Telephone and Telegraph (AT&T)

Telex Machines

Telex is an international message-transfer service for **teleprinter** users. A user attaches a Telex-compatible teleprinter to a Telex line, then dials the person to whom the message is being sent, much like making a telephone call. The recipient's Telex-compatible teleprinter then prints out the message.

Today more than 190 countries use Telex. Sometimes called the first electronic mail service, Telex is the most-used written telecommunication system in the business world.

---

trade name, Teletype. A similar machine was sold at the same time in Germany. Both the American and the German machines used a code originally devised by Emile Baudot for his telegraph. Other teleprinters were developed that used a different keyboard code, the American Standard Code for Information Interchange (ASCII). Commercial teleprinter exchange services, called TRX and Telex, were developed in the 1930s. News wire services became heavy users of teleprinter communications.

Early teletypewriters printed data on strips of gummed tape. Messages on the tape were cut and pasted onto telegram forms. Later machines printed messages in page form. At first, teleprinters produced up to 500 characters per minute. By the mid-1960s, these machines had upped their output to 900 words per minute. Today teleprinters are being replaced by direct transmissions from communication satellites to computers.

⁎⋆⁎ Telescope

Refractor Telescope

The principle of the telescope was first developed by a Dutch spectacle-maker, Hans Lippershey (1570-1619). He used his first telescope, made in 1608, for observing grounded objects from a distance, rather than astronomy. His invention was not openly embraced by the scientific community; he was, in fact, unable to patent it.

In 1609, not far away, Italian mathematics professor **Galileo Galilei** developed his own refractor telescope, without seeing even a model of Lippershey's work. His creation had an object glass that bent light rays to a focus near the eye. There a second **lens,** an eyepiece, magnified the image. His invention grew to be quite popular, as glass was relatively cheap and mirrors of the day were of very poor quality. Galileo's first telescope was small by today's standards and its object glass was only one inch in diameter.

Opposite page: The world's largest refractor-reflector telescope is located at the Mount Palomar Observatory in California. The doors at the top slide open to give a view of the stars.

This simple instrument allowed Galileo to make astonishing discoveries. He saw that the Milky Way comprised thousands of stars, he identified darkened blemishes on the Moon's surface as craters, and he also noted changes (phases) of the Moon's shape. Galileo's instrument was soon enhanced by that of Johannes Kepler (1571-1630), the German astronomer whose creation increased the field of view as well as the magnification pos-

E u r e k a !   *1 0 5 3*

sibilities of the telescope. From their observations, each man was able to derive and confirm a multitude of theories about our solar system.

As refractor telescopes came into wider use, observers realized the instruments had a severe imperfection. Since, like a **prism**, a lens bends different colors of light through different angles, the telescopes produced a false color around any bright object. This defect is called chromatic aberration. One way these early astronomers tried to solve this problem was to create telescopes with extremely long focal length (the distance between the object glass and focus). These were very clumsy instruments to use.

Another solution was the achromatic lens. Chester Moor Hall (1703-1771) constructed the first lens by placing two lenses, made of different kinds of glass, set close together. The false color of one was canceled out by the other; Hall went on to create the achromatic telescope in 1733. The lens itself was further developed by English optician John Dollond (1706-1761) in 1758. His lens combined two or more lenses with varying chemical compositions to minimize the effects of aberration.

Reflector telescopes

Isaac Newton found it more frustrating to create such a lens. Instead, he decided the only solution was to design a telescope that needed no object glass at all. In 1672 he built the first reflector telescope through which light passes down an open tube until it hits a mirror at the lower end. This mirror is curved in such a way to send the light back up the tube, directing it onto a smaller mirror called the diagonal that reflects the light into the eyepiece on the side of the tube. William Herschel used an updated version of this when he discovered **Uranus** in 1781.

Even today, reflectors are perhaps the most prominent type of telescope. They are cost effective, produce little false color, and maintain a high resolution. The mirrors used in larger reflectors, however, often cause distortion due to the weight on the instrument. Newer reflectors are incorporating mirrors of varying shapes (hexagonal glass segments, for example) and are produced using lighter, more durable materials (such as Pyrex). Another option in avoiding this problem is to build several large mirrors, mount them separately on a common base, and link them via computer into one central unit. Some of the largest reflectors are located on Mount Palomar near San Diego, California, and on Mount Pastukhov in Russia.

The latter part of the nineteenth century saw the reappearance of refracting telescopes. What began as a hobby for American astronomer

Alvan Clark ended as a very notable enterprise. For years, Clark had made his own mirrors and lenses. Realizing his were superior to any made in Europe, he set out to manufacture the highest quality lenses possible for sale worldwide. He was successful enough to eventually be given the task of building what was then world's largest refractor: the 36-inch Lick Observatory telescope in California.

After the Lick Observatory telescope's completion in 1887, Clark worked with the University of Southern California in developing an even larger telescope. The university was to buy the lenses and the land was to come from private donation. Unfortunately, due to problems in the real estate market, the project was canceled. Upon hearing of this, George Ellery Hale (inventor of the spectroheliograph used in solar studies) formulated a plan to complete what Clark and the university had begun. Hale worked to secure funding for the project. He struck an agreement with Charles Yerkes, a Chicago railroad millionaire, who fronted over $300,000 for the construction of the world's largest refractor—Yerkes Observatory, which was built in 1897 near Chicago, Illinois. It soon became obvious to Hale that because of resolution flaws and inconsistencies in the resulting images, the size was close to the maximum for a refracting telescope.

Realizing the need for sharper, more distant images, the scientific community turned to the refractor-reflector telescope

Refractor-Reflector Telescope

Realizing the need for sharper, more distant images, the scientific community turned again to the reflector telescope and a new instrument developed by German optician Bernhard Schmidt—the refractor-reflector telescope.

Schmidt invented the first combination refractor-reflector telescope in 1931 for wide-angle astrophotography. It had a thin, specially shaped lens at the end of a tube and a regular mirror at the other end; a photographic plate was also included. The largest Schmidt telescope is located at Palomar Observatory. It can photograph an area of the sky more than 300 times as large as that seen by other reflectors; this is key in mapping the skies and closely studying objects at a significant distance.

The multiple atmospheric layers have hampered telescope observations from Earth's surface. Scientists, therefore, have developed other more efficient means for gathering data on our solar system. These instruments include the **space telescope** and the **solar telescope**.

See also **Communications satellite; Eyeglasses; Navigational satellite; Space probe; Teaching aid; Weather forecasting model**

⁎ Television

About the same time that Guglielmo Marconi was experimenting with **radio** transmissions in the late 1890s, other scientists were exploring the possibility of transmitting pictures. The first inventor to do so was Abbe Caselli, an Italian-born priest who succeeded in sending shadow pictures via the French telegraph lines in 1866.

Almost 20 years later, an Englishman named Shelford Bidwell developed a device that he called an "electric distant vision apparatus." This machine used a **selenium** cell mounted on a box that moved up and down to scan an image.

Nipkow's Device

German scientist Paul Nipkow designed an electric **telescope** that divided its target into scanned lines. Using this as a base, he developed a photomechanical image scanner in 1884 that he called a Nipkow disk. The device was made up of a metal or cardboard disk perforated with a series of square holes in a spiral pattern, so that each hole was slightly closer to the disk's center than the last. As the disk spun, a light was shone through the holes and onto the target. By looking through the holes, one could see the target revealed as a series of horizontal lines.

Though the Nipkow disk became the basis for later photomechanical televisions, technology in the mid-1880s was not advanced enough for Nipkow to pursue his work further. It was Scottish engineer John Logie Baird who eventually continued the research Nipkow had begun.

In 1923 Baird designed a television system using the Nipkow disk. With the addition of a photoelectric cell, Baird's system could read the areas of dim and bright light that made up each scanned line and convert them into an electrical signal. A second Nipkow disk and a flashing light bulb were used to play back the image. A crude but recognizable image was formed when an incoming signal made the bulb flash brightly or dimly, and then synchronized that flashing to the second spinning disk.

Baird's design was used to send coast-to-coast and transatlantic (across the Atlantic Ocean) transmissions during the late 1920s, and it was his device that was first used by the British Broadcasting Company (BBC).

Scientists realized that the photomechanical systems had their limits and an all-electrical device would be far more useful. Several people working over the years contributed partial inventions to what became modern television.

*Few inventions have
had as profound
effect on the world
as television.*

Vladimir Zworykin, Father of Modern TV

The basic model for modern television was designed simultaneously yet independently by two scientists: American Philo Farnsworth and Russian-born American Vladimir Zworykin. Farnsworth demonstrated a working model of his television in 1927, but it was not practical for mass-market production. Farnsworth's investors backed out of the project, and at the onset of World War II (1939-45), the entire project was abandoned.

Zworykin, who is frequently called the "father of television," fared much better than Farnsworth with his invention. After immigrating to the United States in 1919, he found a job with the Westinghouse Electric Corporation. It was there that he developed his iconoscope, an all-electrical television camera.

The iconoscope used a vast array of tiny drops of **selenium**, each acting as an individual photoelectric cell. As the drops were exposed to light, they stored the amount of light they had "seen" as a very small electric pulse. An electron gun was then used to convert the stored pulses into an electric signal that could be transmitted. When the drops' pulses discharged, the process could begin anew and was repeated many times each second.

In 1924, just a year after applying for the patent for his iconoscope, Zworykin developed the kinescope, the forerunner to the modern television receiver. Zworykin's tremendous advances in the field attracted the attention of the Radio Corporation of America (RCA), and in 1929 he began to work for them full-time. It was Zworykin's iconoscope/kinescope system that evolved into the television systems we know today.

Color Comes to Television

In the early years of television, all broadcasts were in black and white. It was not until the late 1950s that a color system was approved. Then a bitter battle ensued between the two largest television companies, RCA and Columbia Broadcasting System (CBS).

CBS was the first to offer a practical color image based upon the work of Peter Goldmark. Goldmark's field-sequential color system delivered color quality unsurpassed even today. Unfortunately, Goldmark's design required all television owners to exchange their existing sets for new field-sequential sets.

RCA offered a color system designed by Ernst Alexanderson. His design was not as clear as the one developed by CBS, but it was compatible with existing black-and-white sets. The Federal Communications Com-

Opposite page: Vladimir Zworykin, the "father of television," holding the cathode-ray receiving tube of the kinescope, the forerunner to the modern television receiver.

How Television Works

Television operates by a principle known as persistence of vision—that is, the human eye is slower than the brain, so if a series of similar images are played rapidly, the brain will blur them together, creating the illusion of animation. This is the same principle by which **motion pictures** work.

Each picture in a standard American television set contains 525 lines. These lines are scanned as you would read a book, starting at the top left and going from left to right and from top to bottom. In the first pass, the scanner shows the odd-numbered lines (1, 3, 5) and then goes back to scan the even-numbered lines (2, 4, 6). This practice helps to decrease screen flicker. In all, it takes just one-thirtieth of a second to scan all 525 lines. This method was adopted in 1951 by the National Television System Committee (NTSC) in order to standardize all American television broadcasts.

mission (FCC) eventually chose to make the RCA color system the industry standard in 1954. (The standards adopted in other countries are not necessarily compatible with American television sets, and digital translators are required in order to receive their images.)

HDTV

The future of television is leaning in the direction of High definition television—also known as HDTV or Hi-Def. The HDTV system offers a much sharper image, comparable to that seen at a movie theater. This is accomplished by transmitting each picture in 1050 lines—twice as many as in a standard television. Because of the increased amount of information transmitted via HDTV, it will probably require two broadcast channels, each containing 525 lines of information. This will most likely be accomplished by using cable television as the broadcast medium.

⋆⋆ Teratogen

A teratogen is any substance that damages the **nervous system** or skeleton in developing human fetuses. The word comes from the Greek *teras,* meaning "monster."

Early Beliefs About Birth Defects

People have wondered what causes birth defects ever since the first malformed baby was born. Early societies believed them to result from the influence of celestial bodies or to be a punishment by the gods. From the seventeenth to the early twentieth centuries, the theory of maternal impression was popular. According to this theory, anything that made a strong impression on the mother during pregnancy would produce a specific birth defect in her child. For instance, a mother who was startled by a hare might give birth to a child with a malformation of the upper lip called a harelip.

During the nineteenth and early twentieth centuries, researchers showed that when lower animals such as chickens and fish were exposed to certain physical and chemical substances, they produced offspring with birth defects. A few medical investigators did studies showing similar effects in mammals. But the scientific community as a whole clung to the

A child who's mother used Thalidomide while she was pregnant. The belief that a woman's placenta prevented harmful substances from reaching the unborn child was shattered by the thalidomide tragedy. We now know that a wide variety of substances— teratogens—can produce birth defects.

belief that a woman's placenta (the sac that holds the fetus during pregnancy) prevented harmful substances from reaching the unborn child. This belief was shattered by the thalidomide tragedy.

Thalidomide

Teratogens cause birth defects in developing human fetuses. The worst teratogen ever developed was thalidomide, which caused birth defects in 5,000 German children and 10,000 children worldwide before it was finally withdrawn from the market.

Thalidomide was a sedative (tranquilizer) and hypnotic drug introduced in West Germany in 1958. At first it was hailed as a "wonder drug" because it quickly sent users into a sound sleep. With no "hangover" effect the following morning and no fatal effects in case of overdose, thalidomide use spread rapidly across Canada and Europe. It was considered so safe that it could be bought "over the counter" in drugstores rather than by prescription.

A year after its introduction, 12 severely deformed infants were born in West Germany. They were affected by a very rare condition called phocomelia, in which the arms and legs developed into stubs resembling a seal's flippers. No link to thalidomide was considered, even after 83 more cases were reported in 1960.

In September 1960 an American drug firm sought permission from the U.S. Food and Drug Administration (FDA) to sell the drug in the United States. The application was given to a new FDA employee, Frances Kelsey, who was expected to approve it within the usual 60 days. Kelsey repeatedly postponed approving the marketing application while she sought further information about the drug.

Meanwhile, cases of phocomelia continued to mount in Europe. Finally, in November 1961, a German pediatrician named Widukind Lenz established that the mothers of many of the infants with severe birth defects at his clinic had taken thalidomide. The link between the drug and birth defects was confirmed in Australia. By the end of November, thalidomide was withdrawn from the market. In the United States, publicity arising from the tragedy brought about a new, landmark law, passed in 1962. The law required much stricter procedures for testing all drugs before they could be sold to the public.

This dramatic proof of the existence of teratogens led to further investigations into the cause of birth defects. We now know that a wide variety of substances can produce birth defects. These include **cocaine** and crack cocaine, alcohol, aspirin, caffeine, cigarette and other types of smoke, food additives, pesticides and herbicides (bug and weed killers), and toxins (poisons) in the workplace. Virtually all drugs, including illegal ones and those sold over the counter or by prescription, have teratogenic possibilities.

When Exposure Does the Most Harm

Researchers have found that damage depends on when the fetus is exposed to the teratogen. For the first two weeks after conception, the developing embryo is relatively unaffected by teratogens. From then until the end of the second month, the rapidly developing organs and body parts are vulnerable to severe malformations from exposure to harmful substances. After that, teratogens can interfere with fetal growth, body function, and brain development.

In the early 1990s, concerns were raised about the effect of teratogens on sperm. Studies have linked fathers' exposure to a number of substances—especially **lead**, pesticides, organic solvents, and heavy metal fumes—to birth defects in their babies. Much more research is certain to be undertaken in this area.

⋆⁎⋆ Tetanus

Tetanus is a serious and often fatal infectious disease caused by **bacteria** that live in the soil. Bacteria called *Clostridium tetani* invade the body through a wound from an object that has the bacteria on it.

The poison produced by these bacteria attack the nerve **cells** in the spinal cord that control muscle activity. After an incubation period (the time before the first symptoms appear) ranging from two days to two weeks, the muscles become rigid, and painful muscle spasms (contractions) can occur.

Looking for a Cure

In 1887 German bacteriologist Emil von Behring was studying disinfectants, substances that destroy, neutralize, or inhibit the growth of disease microorganisms. He noticed that the

Shibasaburo Kitasato was the first to isolate the tetanus bacterium in pure culture in 1889.

blood serum of tetanus-immune laboratory rats neutralized the bacteria that cause anthrax, an infectious disease of warm-blooded animals. He decided to isolate the substance that gave the rats resistance to the anthrax bacteria.

Behring worked with Japanese bacteriologist Shibasaburo Kitasato in the Berlin (Germany) laboratory of scientist Robert Koch. Kitasato was the first to isolate the tetanus bacterium in pure culture in 1889. He later isolated and described the bacteria that cause diphtheria, anthrax, and bubonic plague.

Behring and Kitasato discovered that the presence of tetanus and diphtheria toxins in blood caused the blood to produce antitoxins that neutralize the poisonous substances. When they injected small amounts of tetanus toxin into animals, the antitoxins the animals produced gave them immunity from the disease. Furthermore, if they took blood serum containing antitoxins from these animals and injected it into other animals, the new animals became immune to tetanus as well. They called this procedure "blood serum therapy."

Behring developed a way to produce antitoxin serum in guinea pigs and later developed a toxin-antitoxin mixture that was an effective vaccine against tetanus. In 1893 French scientist Pierre-Paul-Emile Roux, who was the assistant to Louis Pasteur at the Pasteur Institute, developed improved procedures for using antitoxin serum to prevent as well as treat tetanus.

Today the tetanus vaccine is routinely administered to infants in the diphtheria, tetanus, pertussis (whooping cough) (DTP) vaccine. The DTP **inoculation** contains weak toxins that serve to stimulate the growth of antibodies to the diseases. It is given in three shots, administered two months apart, beginning about two months after birth. Booster shots are given at age fifteen months, four to six years, and every ten years thereafter. If a person suffers a dangerous wound, an additional tetanus injection may be needed.

See also **Germ theory; Immune system; Nervous system**

Tetanus is also known as "lockjaw" because the muscle spasms it causes can make it difficult to open one's mouth. Although tetanus was widespread at the turn of the century, it can be prevented today through immunization.

⋆⋆ Thallium

Thallium was discovered by the British physicist William Crookes while he was examining **selenium** and other compounds using a spectroscope.

(A spectroscope is a device for viewing the bands of colored light that combine to make white light.) He noticed a bright, lime-green band that did not correspond to any known element. He named the element "thallium" after the Greek word *thallos* meaning "green twig." At about the same time, this element was isolated by the French chemist C. A. Lamy. Lamy announced his findings shortly after Crookes.

Thallium is normally found as a bluish-gray metal. It is soft enough to be cut with a knife. In its pure form, thallium is dangerous, particularly when in contact with skin. It is often used in electronic equipment. One of its compounds (mixtures), thallium sulfate, is used as a rodent killer and ant poison. Another compound, thallium bromide-iodide, is used in crystal form as an infrared detector.

See also **Spectroscopy**

⋆⋆ 3-D motion picture

3-D is a movie or graphic display seen in three dimensions (height, width, and depth). A viewer sees the picture in more depth and so it seems more "real" than the flatter one- or two-dimensional images.

As early as 1894, attempts were made to enhance **motion pictures** with 3-D special effects. In the early 1900s, 3-D cinema became a reality

A Hollywood audience wearing 3-D glasses screens Bwana Devil, *the first full-length film to use the Polaroid system of filming.*

3-D comic books remain popular with children, who like to wear the special glasses with one red and one green lens.

with the invention of W. E. Waddell's anaglyphic process. This process superimposed twin images (one red, the other green). When the audience viewed the images through special red and green glasses, the two images appeared as one 3-D image.

In 1915 the first commercial 3-D film was shown publicly in New York City and consisted of three black-and-white shorts. The first color movie with sound to use 3-D was released in Germany in 1937. It was made possible by Edwin Herbert Land's development of the Polaroid system of filming. Fifteen years later, American producer Arch Oboler used the Polaroid system to shoot *Bwana Devil,* the first feature (full-length) film to use the Polaroid system. Oboler used two cameras whose reels were synchronized (they ran at the same rate). Spectators had to wear Polaroid glasses to get the 3-D effect. A short-lived 3-D fad resulted, with more than 100 films produced this way.

Despite improvements in the making of 3-D films, many viewers disliked wearing the special glasses. So 3-D films have remained a novelty.

⁎ Time zone

As Earth rotates on its axis from west to east, night and day arrive at different parts of Earth at different times. Until the late 1800s, every town, county, or isolated group of islands observed its own time and set **clocks** according to the local sunrise and sunset. Time differences between locations did not really matter to people anyway, because it took time to travel any great distance, and there were no instant modes of communication to cause confusion about what time it actually was.

Demand for a unified time system evolved as a result of two technological advances: the telegraph and the **train**. In the 1830s, the telegraph made possible instantaneous communication between distant points. The first trains, developed in England and America, made rapid travel possible. With the development of telegraph and railroad networks on a continental scale in North America, Europe, and elsewhere, local times came into conflict. It was nearly impossible to create schedules or to relay messages efficiently. Railroads wrote timetables, but these schedules were not coordinated among the railroad companies in different locations. So, you might set out by train following a schedule that had no relation to the schedule used at your destination.

Cleveland Abbe to the Rescue

American meteorologist Cleveland Abbe, who helped found the U.S. Weather Bureau in 1870, pioneered a system of weather reporting and forecasting and used the telegraph to collect and distribute information. Accurate timekeeping was necessary for accurate weather forecasting, so by 1883 Abbe had persuaded North American railroads to adopt time zones.

The following year, an international system of 24 time zones was adopted. The line of 0° longitude, which runs through the Greenwich Observatory at London, England, is the prime, or starting, meridian. The zones extending east from Greenwich (toward the European continent) increase one hour each for a total of 12 hours. The zones extending west (across the Atlantic Ocean) decrease by a total of 12 hours. The 24th zone (in the Pacific Ocean) is divided by the International Date Line, at 180° longitude. The time difference on either side of the line is 24 hours, one day greater west of the line than east of it.

There are problems with this idealized time zone system. For instance, Newfoundland and the Cook Islands are located in half-hour zones. In the former Soviet Union, all time zones are one hour greater than the zones adopted in 1884. Time zone boundaries, especially in populated areas, are purposely defined along political (country) boundaries or physical features (such as mountains). Even the International Date Line, which runs down the center of the Pacific Ocean, has been bent through the Bering Strait so that Siberia and Alaska are entirely within their own time units.

Time zones of the world. Before time zones were initiated, you might set out on a train trip using a schedule that was not followed at your destination.

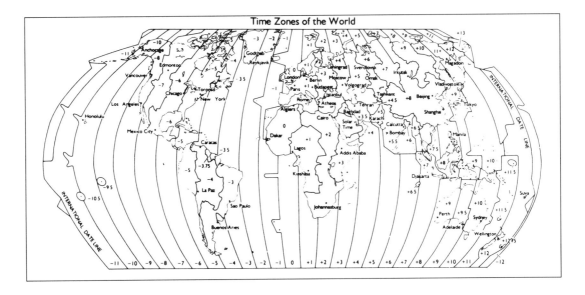

Time Zones of the World

⁺ Tin

The canned foods we buy today are packaged in containers made of aluminum lined with tin. But for a long time after English inventor Peter Durand created the "tin canister" in 1810, all cans were made of tin. In fact, many people still refer to cans as "tin cans."

Tin is a silver-white metal with a bluish tint. It is found mainly in cassiterite (SnO_2), an ore. Bolivia is the world's primary producer of tin. Other deposits are found in Malaysia, Indonesia, Thailand, Zaire, and Nigeria. There are no significant deposits in the United States.

Uses

Tin was known and prized in ancient times. Its earliest use was as an alloy (mixture) with copper in bronze. A small amount of tin added to copper makes the mixture harder and more malleable (easily bent), so the mixture is more practical than pure copper for making tools and weapons.

Tin is also alloyed with copper and antimony (another metal) to make pewter. Pewter is very easily worked and was popular for use in pots and dinnerware from the thirteenth century through the early nineteenth century.

The canned foods we buy today are packaged in containers made of aluminum lined with tin.

Tin is currently used as a soft solder (pronounced sod-der; solders are the equivalent of a metal glue). It is often used as a coating for other metals to retard corrosion (wearing out or rusting). It is used to coat the inside of cans used for preserving food (tin does not affect the food inside the can). Until recently, tin-plated **iron** or steel was used as a roofing material, especially in the Midwestern United States. "Tin roofs" had a reputation for durability. Nowadays, however, zinc-plated metal roofs are more common, although they are still often referred to as "tin roofs."

Tin salts are used for panel lighting and frost-free windshields in **automobiles**. A new alloy of tin and niobium, a rare metal used in jewelry and industry, has proven to be useful in the creation of superconductive magnets, which use a fraction of the power needed in standard electromagnets.

See also **Electromagnetism**

⋆⋆ Tissue

Tissues are groups of similar **cells** that perform a common function necessary for an organism's survival. All complex animals and plants (multicellular organisms) have tissues. Tissue groups include epithelial (skin and digestive), muscular, nervous, connective, and vascular (**blood**).

Though it was obvious to very early scientists that organisms consist of many types of body parts, they did not possess the technology (such as microscopes) to examine bodily components closely. They based their studies of anatomy (body parts) on obvious characteristics such as the location of organs. No scientist made an effort to classify body parts according to what they did (function) or what they were made of (structure).

In the 1700s, the term "tissue," from the French *tisser,* began to be used in anatomical science in recognition of the fine textures that made

The study of tissues is called histology.

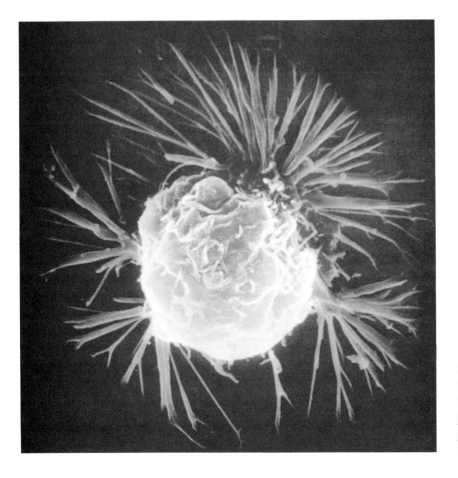

Breast cancer tissue. Because each tissue has specific properties, it is also prone to specific diseases.

various bodily components different from one another. French anatomist Xavier Bichat (1771-1802) was perhaps the first to fully consider the body of an organism with reference to tissues.

What Bichat Found

Bichat, working without a microscope, found that organs were built up out of different types of simpler structures. Each of these simpler structures could occur in more than one organ. Bichat observed that because each tissue had specific properties, it was also prone to specific diseases. He suggested adopting a systematic order for anatomy, instead of an order that described the location of body parts. Bichat listed 21 tissues (or systems) in the human body based on what he saw during his postmortem (after death) examinations. He distinguished the different tissues by their composition and by the arrangement of their fibers.

Histology (the study of tissues) began to take on its modern form when German histologist Theodor Schwann introduced cell theory in 1839. It was then that tissues began to be understood not as the basic building blocks of living things, but as unique systems of cells with distinct origins.

⋆⋆⋆ Titanium

The atomic number of titanium is 22, its atomic weight is 47.90, and its chemical symbol Ti. Titanium dioxide is the whitest known pigment.

Titanium is an element occurring as a bright, lustrous, brittle metal or a dark gray powder. It is the ninth most common element in Earth's crust and is widely found in igneous rocks (molten rock that becomes solid). Titanium has also been found in **meteorites**, in moon rocks, and in the **Sun** and other stars.

The first mention of titanium appears in the writings of an English clergyman and amateur scientist, William Gregor. In 1791 Gregor described his analysis of a mineral found in a valley in Cornwall. He reported that the mineral contained a "reddish brown calx" that he could not identify and that he thought might include "a new metallic substance." Gregor's report was printed in a European journal. It was largely ignored and his discovery was forgotten until 1795, when German chemist Martin Heinrich Klaproth decided to re-study it.

Klaproth concluded that Gregor had indeed found a new element. Klaproth suggested the name "titanium" after the Titans, the first sons of the earth according to Greek mythology.

Uses

The most important use of titanium is in alloys (metal mixtures). Titanium alloys are very strong considering their weight and can withstand great changes in temperature. These properties make them valuable in the manufacture of parts for airplanes and spacecraft.

Titanium's resistance to salt water has made it useful in alloys used in propeller blades and ship parts. The same property suggests a possible use in desalinizing systems, which remove the salt from water.

Titanium dioxide, TiO_2, is the most widely used compound of the element. Since TiO_2 is nontoxic, it has become the most popular pigment in white paint since the use of lead compounds in paints was discontinued. Titanium dioxide is also used as a coloring in foods, ceramics, plastics, inks, and enamels, and as a filler and coater in paper. Titanium tetrachloride liquid reacts with ammonia to produce large volumes of smoke, and is used in **skywriting**.

✦ Toaster

In the twentieth century people have become more adept at using energy sources such as gas and electricity. The average kitchen is a prime example of this efficiency. Take the electric toaster, for instance. It is one of the most common appliances in American households.

While a few prototypes (first versions) appeared before 1900, the first models marketed to the public were those invented by the General Electric Company of Schenectady, New York, in 1909. These early toasters were simply strips of bare wire wound around mica strips. (Mica is a mineral found in igneous rocks.) The wire was heated by electrical current, and the mica strips spread the heat evenly over the bread.

The first toaster that could heat both sides of the bread appeared in 1927. It included a clock-like mechanism and spring that would cut off the toaster's power and release the toasted bread. In the early 1930s, further enhancements were made by adding a thermostat that would shut off the toaster's power when the bread reached a certain temperature. In 1932, the spring mechanism of the toaster was perfected and soon after pop-up toasters became common sights in kitchens across America.

Toasted bread used to be prepared over an open fire, much like we roast hot dogs today.

⋆⋆⋆ Toilet

People have long sought an efficient method of disposing of human waste. The earliest known flush toilet dates from 1800 B.C. It was installed in the royal palace at Knossos in Crete. It had a wooden seat and used a drainage system with venting air shafts. Water-flushed latrines (communal toilets) were in use in the Indus Valley near Tibet around 2500 to 1500 B.C. By the fourth century A.D. the Romans used them too. The flush toilet then disappeared for many centuries. Instead, chamber pots became the norm in Europe during the Middle Ages (A.D. 400-1450). These were emptied into public streets.

The idea of the flush toilet was finally revived around 1590 by the godson of Queen Elizabeth I of England, Sir John Harington. He designed

Guests at the lavish French palace of Versailles were forced to relieve themselves behind bushes and statues on the grounds. Plumbing and sewage systems were primitive or nonexistent at the time it was built in 1661.

and had installed in his home a water closet. It had an overhead water tank with a valve that released water on demand. Although the queen had one of her godson's inventions installed in her palace, the water closet did not catch on.

Drainage and venting problems made these early toilets unsanitary and bad smelling. Plumbing and sewage systems were primitive or non-existent. Even at the lavish French palace of Versailles (built in 1661), residents and guests had to relieve themselves outdoors among the statuary and shrubbery.

Water Closet Advances

Water closet design advanced no further until English watchmaker Alexander Cummings patented a version with an improved valve in 1775. British cabinetmaker Joseph Bramah patented a design with an even better hinged valve in 1778. Toilets then began to come into common use in England. The major problem of disposing of their contents remained. Water closets typically drained into cesspools. A cesspool is a collection pit. Pipes in these cesspools usually leaked eventually, fouling the surrounding soil. Drainage into sewer systems usually resulted in discharge into a nearby river, polluting the drinking water supply.

These problems were solved with the invention of the septic system in the mid-1800s and the practice of treating sewage before discharging it. London had a modern sewage system by the 1860s. That year, Bramah's water closet design was improved by London plumber Thomas Crapper, who added an automatic flush shutoff and lent his last name as an English slang word for the word "toilet."

Flush Toilets Come to America

Flush toilets only came into use in the United States after 1870, and then slowly, because so many homes lacked running water. The outhouse or privy, backed up by the chamber pot for nighttime use, remained standard in both rural America and in tenements (rental dwellings) well into the twentieth century.

Gayetty's Medicated Paper was the first modern—that is, soft—toilet paper. It was introduced by New Yorker Joseph C. Gayetty in 1857. Toilet paper in rolls was the contribution of Philadelphia brothers E. Irvin and Clarence Scott in 1879.

The British were responsible for the development of modern toilets, while to the Americans goes the credit for the invention of toilet paper.

⋆⋆ Toothbrush and toothpaste

Early Brushes

The earliest toothbrushes were simply small sticks mashed at one end to increase their cleaning surface. Ancient Roman aristocrats employed special slaves to clean their teeth. Brushing the teeth was part of some ancient religious observances.

The bristle brush was probably invented by the Chinese, and it came to Europe during the seventeenth century. French dentists, who were then the most advanced in Europe, advocated the use of toothbrushes in the seventeenth and early eighteenth centuries. Dentists urged pre-Revolutionary War Americans to use bristle toothbrushes.

Nylon has replaced the natural bristles used by the Chinese in toothbrushes. Modern toothpaste has replaced cleaning compounds that once included ingredients such as mice, lizard livers, and urine.

Modern Brushes

Dr. Scott's Electric Toothbrush was marketed in 1880. Its manufacturer claimed the brush was "permanently charged with electro-magnetic current." The first real electric toothbrush was developed in Switzerland after World War II (1939-45). This model, complete with electric cord, was introduced to the United States market in 1960 by the Squibb company under the name Broxodent. General Electric followed in 1961 with its rechargeable cordless model. Although it seemed an odd idea to many people at the time, the electric toothbrush was an immediate success.

Toothpaste

Like toothbrushes, compounds for cleaning teeth (and freshening breath) have been used since ancient times. Early Egyptian, Chinese, Greek, and Roman writings describe numerous mixtures for both pastes and powders. The more appetizing ingredients included powdered fruit, burnt shells, talc, honey, ground shells, and dried flowers. The less appetizing ingredients included mice, the head of a hare, lizard livers, and urine. Powder and paste formulas continued to multiply through the Middle Ages (A.D. 400-1450). Unfortunately, many of these recipes used ingredients that corroded (wore down) or abraded (nicked) the non-replaceable tooth enamel.

Modern toothpastes began to appear in the 1800s. Soap was added to tooth cleaners in 1824. Chalk was popularized by John Harris in the 1850s, and soon the then well-known S. S. White Company introduced a paste in a collapsible tube. Washington W. Sheffield, a Connecticut dentist, put his popular Dr. Sheffield's Creme Dentifrice in its collapsible tube on the market in 1892. The toothpaste tube reigned supreme until 1984. Then the pump dispenser, which originated in Europe, was introduced to the U.S. market. Fluoride, a chemical to fight tooth decay, was added to toothpaste in 1956, when Procter & Gamble launched its Crest product.

⁎⋆ Topology

In the mid-eighteenth century, Swiss mathematician Leonhard Euler became fascinated by a puzzle. The ancient Prussian (German) city of Königsberg (King's City) contained seven bridges. According to a tradition among the residents of Königsberg, it was impossible to walk over all seven bridges without crossing one of them at least twice. Euler devised an entirely new branch of mathematics, now known as topology, to solve the puzzle.

Topology is a field of geometry that examines changes that occur in an object when it is stretched, bent, twisted, or otherwise deformed in some way. It is different from other forms of mathematics because it deals with shapes rather than metrics (distances and angles, for example). It is thus primarily qualitative rather than quantitative in nature.

Combinatorial Topology

Two forms of topology exist. One, combinatorial topology, is also known as "rubber-sheet" geometry. Problems such as that of the Königsberg bridges involve a practical form of combinatorial topology known as network theory. The second form of topology is point set topology.

The Dutch mathematician Luitzen Egbertus Jan Brouwer (1881-1966) has since shown how the two branches of topology can be combined into a single generalized subject.

Euler's research on topological problems was largely ignored for a century. German mathematician Johann Benedict Listing was the first to use the term "topology" in his book, *Vorstudien zur topologie*. Listing's book is regarded by many historians as the first systematic treatment of topology.

The science of topology was devised to solve the riddle of the ancient Prussian city of Königsberg: Why was it impossible to walk over all of the city's seven bridges without crossing one of them at least twice?

One of the most
intriguing
consequences of
topological
studies has
been the
development of
catastrophe
theory, the
attempt to
explain
processes that
occur as a
series of
sudden,
intermittent
events.

Two of the most famous topological figures were developed by the German mathematicians August Ferdinand Möbius (1790-1868) and Christian Felix Klein (1849-1925). Möbius described a method for making a paper strip with only one side, while Klein extended this concept to three dimensions, showing how to produce a bottle with no inside.

For some historians of mathematics, the real beginnings of topology as a field of mathematics can be traced to a the work of Jules-Henri Poincaré (1854-1912). Poincaré's book, *Analysis situs,* and other works outlined many of the concepts that are still fundamental to topological studies today.

Point Set Topology

In point set topology, geometric figures are regarded as discrete (distinct and separate) subsets of a structured space. The beginnings of point set topology can be traced to the work first of the French mathematician Maurice-René Fréchet (1878-1973) and later to that of the German mathematician Felix Hausdorff (1868-1942). Fréchet laid important groundwork by describing a method for determining the distance between any two points in abstract space, thereby defining the concept of metric space.

Hausdorff's most productive work dealt with topology and set theory. He built on Fréchet's concepts, showing how geometric spaces can be regarded as sets of points and sets of relationships among points. His book, *Grundzüge der Mengenlehre* (1910) is now regarded as the classic work about point-set topology.

The study of topology has mushroomed. It has gradually become apparent that the concepts of topology may form a basis for unifying many aspects of mathematical theory. The American mathematician Luther Eisenhart (1876-1965), for example, showed how topology is related to differential geometry. The Polish-born American Samuel Eilenberg developed techniques for using the methods of algebra to deal with problems in topology. The Russian mathematician Pavel Sergeevich Aleksandrov (1896-1982) applied the principles of solid geometry to topology and has contributed to the field of topology known has homology.

Catastrophe Theory

One of the most intriguing consequences of topological studies has been the development of catastrophe theory. Catastrophe theory tries to describe and eventually explain processes that occur as a series of sudden, discontinuous (intermittent) events. In the mid-1950s, the French mathematician René Thom found that such events can often be described by using techniques from topology.

British mathematician Erik Christopher Zeeman also made important contributions to the development of catastrophe theory. This application of topology is particularly exciting and important since it promises to find application in many practical problems in physics, chemistry, biology, and other sciences.

⋆⋆ Torpedo

Torpedoes in History

The torpedo is named after a fish similar to a ray that gives an electric shock. The first torpedo was an underwater explosive charge (what are

A machinist-inspector measures torpedo rear sections during World War II.

now called mines). The same name was also given to explosive charges attached to lines and towed by boats. This type of torpedo was used in the American Civil War (1861-65) by the Confederate submersible vessel *H. L. Hunley* to sink the Union ship U.S.S. *Housatonic* in 1864.

The modern torpedo appeared in 1865. An Austrian military man devised a boat-shaped craft driven by a clockwork device and guided by lines attached to its rudder. It was, in effect, a small electric boat containing an explosive and steered from shore. However, this vehicle was too difficult to operate effectively.

Robert Whitehead (1823-1905), the British manager of a marine engine factory in Austria, developed a much better torpedo. His design was an underwater missile driven by a compressed-air engine. It traveled at a speed of six knots (a knot is about 1.15 miles per hour) for a few hundred yards, carrying an explosive charge of 18 pounds of **dynamite** in its head. Whitehead demonstrated his invention to the British navy. A British ship used one of his torpedoes in action in an 1877 battle.

Many improvements to the basic design followed. In World War II (1939-45), the Germans developed an electrically driven torpedo that proved impossible to track back to its launching **submarine**, unlike the steam-powered ones that left bubbles in their path.

Torpedoes Today

Modern torpedoes are impressive weapons. The U.S. Navy has a 21-inch diameter design that is driven at high speeds using hydrogen peroxide for its fuel. The navy also has Subroc, a device fired as a torpedo deep below the surface. It emerges from the water, flies like a guided missile, moves on an interception course toward its target, submerges again, acts as a homing torpedo (acts as if it can "see" its target), and finally explodes near the enemy like a depth charge.

Many torpedoes incorporate passive or active homing systems or wire guidance that work with the electronic sensors. Tiny torpedoes have been developed for launching from **helicopters**. An antisubmarine rocket (ASROC) launches a rocket-propelled ballistic missile containing an acoustic-homing torpedo.

See also **Artillery; Clock and watch; Rocket and missile; Submarine**

✦ Traffic signal

Ever since the Romans built their massive system of roads 2,000 years ago, society has tried to control traffic. The Roman road system created a conflict between pedestrians and equine (horse-mounted) travelers. A practical solution was not developed until 1868. That year, J. P. Knight, a railway signaling engineer, created the first traffic signal, which was installed near Westminster Abbey in London, England. Unfortunately, the device exploded, killing a police officer, and its use was discontinued.

The modern traffic light was invented in America. By 1918 New York City had a three-color system that was operated manually from a tower in the middle of the street. Other cities soon adopted the idea of having someone on the scene to control the lights. Garrett Morgan, inventor of the **gas mask**, also developed traffic signaling devices. His electric traffic light system consisted of a pole on which the words "stop" and "go" were illuminated. It was patented in 1923.

In 1926 the first automatic signals were installed in London, England. They depended on a timer to activate them. In the 1930s vehicle-activated lights were created. Cars would roll over half-buried rubber tubes. The weight of the cars displaced the air in the tubes. The increased pressure operated an electric contact, which then activated the lights. But these tubes wore out quickly.

The modern traffic light was invented in America. By 1918 New York City had a three-color system.

A better idea was the inductive-loop device. A loop of wire was imbedded in the road and was connected to a box controlling the lights. A current of electricity passed through the loop. When the steel body of a car passed overhead, it produced a signal that activated the light.

Today, researchers in government, industry, and universities are working together to create an Intelligent Vehicle Highway System or IVHS. In this system, sensors alongside the road will communicate with sensors inside the vehicles. These sensors will control vehicle speed and direction. The onboard **computer** in the car can then select the best route to a destination by using the updated information just received from the roadside transmitters.

⋆⋆⋆ Train and railroad

Evolution of the Rail

When the first practical steam locomotive was invented in the early 1800s, transportation consisted of ships for open water travel and barges, for inland travel, pulled by horses that walked alongside the canals. Stage coaches and horsedrawn wagons also transported passengers and cargo, but on shorter runs.

Before the Civil War began in 1861, the American rail network covered 30,000 miles. By the end of the century, more than 200,000 miles of track were largely responsible for opening the western half of the country to settlement.

A number of inventors, including James Watt (1736-1819), John Stevens (1749-1838), and his son Robert (1787-1856), aided in the development of **steam engines**. This work eventually led to the introduction in 1804 of Richard Trevithick's steam locomotive.

Other inventors concentrated on creating better tracks for the new steam-powered trains. In 1821 John Birkinshaw perfected a method of rolling wrought-iron rails. These rolled rails withstood extreme weight and required fewer joints. English rail engineer George Stephenson laid Birkinshaw's rolled rails on England's Stockton and Darlington Railway (S&D). The S&D railway was originally planned as a horse-powered, wooden rail road. Stephenson's laying of iron track and the use of some steam locomotives demonstrated for the first time some of the advantages of steam power over horses. When Stephenson's Liverpool and Manchester railway branch (L&M) opened in the late 1820s, it was the first railway in the world to rely exclusively on steam locomotion. It was also the fastest and most reliable line to that date.

Railway madness had begun in Europe. English rail projects had proven the feasibility and profitability of land transport by steam. By the mid-1800s, England's rail companies were employing 250,000 construction workers, nearly 10,000 miles (16,090 km) of railroads had been laid, and investments exceeded £250,000,000.

Railroads Come to America

Railway madness arrived about the same time in America. The Delaware and Hudson Railroad opened in 1829 with the imported locomotive Stourbridge Lion at its head. Another foreign locomotive, the John Bull, served the Camden and Amboy Rail-Road and Transportation Company (C&A) in New Jersey. It had been built in England and was shipped disassembled. When it arrived in 1831, it was put together by a teenage boy named Isaac Dripps, who added a distinctly American feature: the cowcatcher. The cowcatcher is an iron frame that projects from the front of the locomotive and clears the track of obstructions.

Robert Stevens, who was instrumental in the development of the steam engine, was in charge of laying the track for the C&A. At the time, rails were anchored directly onto stone blocks. Stevens laid a bed of crushed rocks instead of the stone blocks. On top he placed a series of wooden cross ties to which the rails were anchored. His design provided a smoother ride for passengers and helped absorb and distribute the loco-motive's weight. This technique has been used for virtually every rail since placed.

The Baltimore and Ohio Railway (B&O) used Peter Cooper's small Tom Thumb (1830) to prove that steam locomotives could compete with canals and horse teams even on curvy and hilly track. The Tom Thumb was the first locomotive to pull a load of passengers in America. In 1831 the B&O announced a contest for designing a lightweight locomotive that could reach a speed of 15 mph (24 kph) and pull a load of 15 tons (13.6 t) on level ground. Phineas Davis's York won the contest.

Other engineering improvements were made. The vertical design gave way to horizontal engines that improved speed and traction (ability

Man and machine laying track. Robert Stevens, who was in charge of laying the track for the C&A railroad, was the first to place a series of wooden cross ties to which the rails were anchored over a bed of crushed rocks.

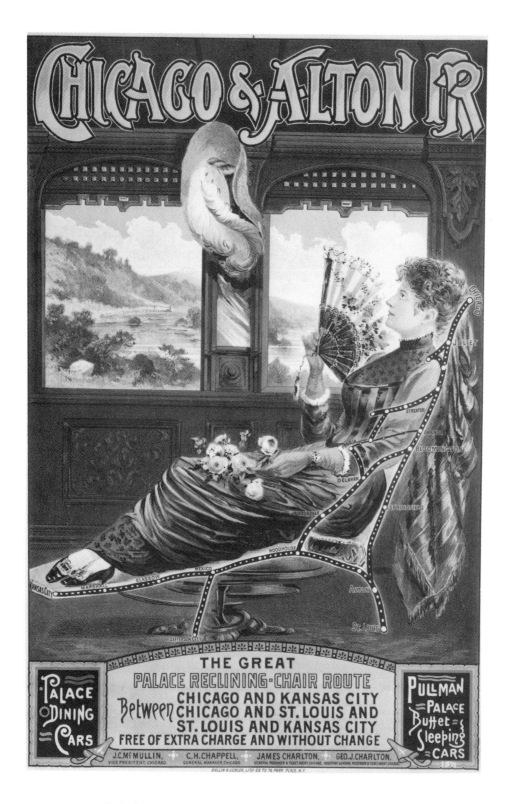

to stay on track). Switches allowed trains to change directions. They became possible when curves and grades were improved as companies acquired more direct rights-of-way and dug **tunnels**, built **bridges**, and made turns more gradual.

Passengers Demand Speed, Comfort, Safety

Railways had been envisioned originally as a method for moving freight. However, in spite of catastrophic accidents in the early days of rail transportation, people began to seek passage on them. At first, passengers sat on wooden benches in open wagons. Those who could afford to travel first class sat in their own carriages, which were attached to a flat bed car. As rail lines spread across the country, people began to demand higher speeds, greater efficiency, and more comfort.

In the mid-1800s, George Pullman began making sleeping and dining cars. These cars still resembled stagecoaches. They were crowded, filled with smoke and ash from both the engine and car heaters, and tended to jump and rock. Pullman's 1864 Pioneer led the change in attitude and design, and before long his cars were in such demand, even in Europe, that he built large manufacturing facilities near Chicago.

With staggering increases in rail traffic, safety devices became more necessary. Derailments, especially on sharp curves, were largely solved by the invention of swiveling wheel trucks by Horatio Allen, John B. Jervis, and Ross Winans. Hitching rail cars together (coupling) remained a dangerous job for railroad workers into the middle of the nineteenth century until better designed coupling mechanisms and systems were introduced. Claude Chappe's manual signaling system became widely adopted. Once the telegraph became common, it was used for sending location messages. George Westinghouse contributed greatly to brake system safety with his pressure (1868) and later vacuum (1872) brakes.

Before the Civil War began in 1861, the American rail network covered 30,000 miles (48,270 km). By the end of the century, more than 200,000 miles (321,800 km) of track were largely responsible for opening the western half of the country to settlement.

Twentieth-Century Trains

While twentieth-century developments in rail transportation have not been as dramatic or important as what went before, some advancements continue to be made. For example, after little change in track technology for many decades, continuous welded rails became common after 1950,

Opposite page: An advertisement for the Chicago & Alton railroad. As rail lines spread across the country, people began to demand higher speeds, greater efficiency, and more comfort.

providing improved safety, reduced noise, and lower maintenance. Since the 1960s, lower-friction and more maintenance-free types of track and bases using concrete have been developed.

Current technology allows for eliminating rails altogether. In 1958 engineers began experimenting with TACVs (tracked air-cushion vehicles). Like hovercrafts, TACVs would not need rails at all and could operate faster and more smoothly since they ride on a cushion of air rather than a guideway. Another related high-speed option is magnetic levitation, or MAGLEV technology, in which an electromagnetic charge on the underside of a vehicle repels the opposite charge on the top of a support. Traveling about 4 inches (10.2 cm) above its guides, one prototype has demonstrated a speed of 321 miles per hour (516.5 kph), a world "rail" speed record. Both of these technologies have been tested in Europe, Japan, and the United States.

Fuels are a current research focus. While diesel engines are still the most common power source in the United States, trains, buses, and other electric-powered vehicles are increasingly used in cities.

The Union Pacific yard in Salt Lake City, Utah.

Duorail, or two-rail, systems have dominated the railway scene since the beginning. Today, however, monorail, or single-rail, systems have interested some inventors. While the first monorail system (drawn by horses) was patented in 1821 by English engineer Henry Palmer, it was not until the later part of the twentieth century that commercially safe and successful monorail systems were built. Modern monorail systems usually operate in urban or commercial areas and frequently use rubber tires for smoother, quieter rides.

A French-built electric "bullet" train can reach speeds of up to 136 miles per hour (218.8 kph).

⋆⋆⋆ Trampoline

George Nissen, the man who invented the trampoline, was a creative inventor who knew how to promote and sell his products. Nissen first got the idea for the trampoline by watching circus high wire and trapeze artists. He noticed that some artists continued to perform in the safety nets, doing twists, spins, and somersaults rather than simply jumping to the ground as quickly as possible.

Nissen took over his family's garage in Cedar Rapids, Iowa, in 1926, and began work on his version of a "bouncing table." Although the idea for such a table was not new, Nissen wanted to improve on the design of those that already existed. He hunted for materials for it—springs, rubber inner tubes, and scraps of iron—at the town dump and anywhere else he could find them. Somehow he came upon an industrial sewing machine and adapted it to sew rubber.

It was important that the table be simple to transport, set up, and store. It had to be large and strong enough to withstand various types of jumping safely, but it had to take up a minimum amount of floor space.

When Nissen graduated from college in 1938, he set to work perfecting and promoting his invention. He even invented the machines necessary to mass produce the table. He then strapped the finished product to the top of his car and left on a cross-country tour. He demonstrated his invention wherever crowds gathered. He used the profits from the first sales to purchase advertising in various sports magazines.

Nissen enlisted in the U.S. Navy during World War II (1939-45) and persuaded both the army and navy to use his invention in their pilot training programs. After the war he expanded his promotional touring to include Europe. He used a kangaroo to prove that users of his invention could outjump it.

By 1948 colleges and universities had added trampolining to their gymnastics competitions. The feeling of weightlessness that the trampoline simulates was useful to America's training astronauts. In 1964 the trampoline volleyball game "Spaceball" swept the country. Nissen's company (which no longer exists) branched out into production of all sorts of gymnastics, **basketball**, and scoreboard equipment, which was sold mainly to schools and colleges.

⋆⋆ Tranquilizer (antipsychotic type)

Tranquilizers are substances that produce a state of calmness in agitated people. **Barbiturates** are minor tranquilizers used in the treatment of anxiety (fearfulness). Major tranquilizers are also known as antipsychotics. They can alleviate symptoms of major psychotic illnesses such as schizophrenia. In psychotic illnesses, normal thinking and the ability to function with other people deteriorate to the point where the afflicted person withdraws from reality. Antipsychotics slow patients down and provide them with emotional serenity (calmness) and an indifference to events occurring around them.

Major Tranquilizers in France

Major tranquilizers (antipsychotics) were first used in France in the early 1950s. The French used major tranquilizers on patients undergoing surgery in order to calm their fears.

Phenothiazines

Phenothiazines differ from barbiturates not only in their medical uses and behavioral effects, but also in their level of toxicity (poisonous effect). It is almost impossible to overdose on major tranquilizers. However, an overdose of barbiturates can cause total respiratory arrest. Side effects also distinguish tranquilizers from barbiturates. These side effects always come with therapeutic (medicinal) use of the drugs, and include increased heart rate, dry mouth, blurred vision, and constipation.

A drug called Phenergan was found to increase the effect brought on by barbiturates used during **anesthesia**. Phenergan is a member of the phenothiazine family, the largest class of antipsychotic drugs.

A tranquilizer called chlorpromazine was found to reduce the amount of anesthetic needed in surgery without bringing on loss of consciousness itself. It appeared to profoundly alter patients' mental awareness, making them quiet and sedate, yet still conscious and apparently uninterested in the events occurring around them.

These effects led doctors to try chlorpromazine in the treatment of mental illness, which resulted in the discovery that the drug relieved psychotic episodes (which occur when a person loses touch with reality). For the first time a drug had been discovered that targeted the central **nervous system** without profoundly affecting other behavioral or motor functions.

Tranquilizers in America

After becoming popular in France, chlorpromazine was marketed in the United States in 1954. It soon became widely used as a treatment for psychotic patients in mental institutions.

Reserpine

American doctors also tested a drug called Reserpine on mentally ill patients. They observed that their patients were able to participate in activities instead of becoming sleepy with increased doses.

Reserpine and other tranquilizers reduce the fear, hostility, agitation, delusions, and hallucinations experienced by seriously mentally ill people. (When healthy people take these drugs, however, they experience slower thinking and response times.)

The use of Reserpine for psychotic patients steadily decreased despite its initial promising results. It had a tendency to produce a number of side effects such as reduced blood pressure, diarrhea, and depression.

In the 1960s, Belgian scientists developed a class of drugs that later became available in the United States under the names haloperidol (Halol) and droperidol (Inapsine). These drugs have provided alternatives for patients who cannot tolerate drugs such as Phenergan.

Unlike minor tranquilizers, major tranquilizers of the antipsychotic type are not addictive and patients generally do not build up a tolerance to them. Therefore, psychotic patients can take them for years without increasing their dosage.

✦ Transmutation of elements

Alchemy

Many chemistry textbooks open with a brief description of alchemy, a very early form of chemistry. A major goal of alchemy was to find a method for transmuting elements (changing one element into another).

Some forms of alchemy probably existed in most ancient civilizations. It may have reached Western Europe from the Arab world, by way of North Africa and the Moorish occupation of Spain between A.D. 700 and 1500.

Wherever it occurred, alchemy was based on a common philosophy, namely that the ability to become perfect was possible in all things, living and non-living. This view was expressed in the belief, for example, that metals grow within the earth ("Mother Earth"), just as plants and animals grow. **Lead**, **tin**, and **iron** were thought to be primitive metals that, if left alone in the earth, would eventually grow to make "mature" metals such as copper, **silver**, and, finally, the most perfect of all metals, **gold**.

Alchemy tried to find ways to make that process occur more quickly. Alchemists searched for a "philosopher's stone," some material that could be used to convert base metals, such as lead, into gold. They had a similar objective with regard to human life. In this case, they searched for an "elixir of life" that could be used to cure any disease or illness and guarantee eternal life.

Where "Alchemy" Comes From

The origin of the term "alchemy" is uncertain. The prefix *al-* is a definite article in Arabic meaning "the," while *-chem* may come from early French, German, Greek, Arabic, or Egyptian terms that refer to the study of materials or the alloying (mixing) of metals.

Scientists found that radioactivity was a process by which one element gives off some form of radiation as it changes into a new element.

Both objectives had great appeal to the general population and to the nobility. Nearly every ruler maintained a court alchemist whose job it was to achieve great wealth and/or eternal life for the patron.

Most of the thoughts and practices of alchemists is shrouded in mystery. They wrote about their ideas and experiments in mysterious language so no one would learn of any great discoveries they might make.

Contributions to Modern Chemistry

Neither the philosopher's stone nor the elixir of life was ever found. But alchemists made important contributions to the development of modern chemistry. First, they invented research techniques and instruments that were eventually used by the first modern chemists. Among these instruments and techniques were different kinds of containers used to melt materials at high temperatures; mortars and pestles (devices for grinding substances into powder); and furnaces and other equipment for distilling, crystallizing, smelting (fusing), and alloying. Furthermore, alchemists discovered five new elements—antimony, arsenic, bismuth, **phosphorus**, and zinc—as well as a number of new compounds (mixtures).

Birth of Modern Chemistry

By the eighteenth century, alchemy had largely died out in Europe. Modern chemists no longer took seriously the belief that one element could be changed into another. Indeed, one of the basic principles of modern chemistry was that matter was *stable*. Elements were not expected to change into other elements, with or without the help of Mother Earth or chemists.

Until the twentieth century, most chemists scoffed at the concept of transmutation. Then, late in the nineteenth century, evidence began to accumulate that transmutation might not be such an absurd idea after all. In 1896 French physicist Antoine-Henri Becquerel discovered the phenomenon of

British physicist Ernest Rutherford was the first to transmute one element (nitrogen) into another element (oxygen).

radioactivity. Over the following two decades, scientists found that radioactivity was a process by which one element gives off some form of radiation as it changes into a new element.

Intrigued by this discovery, scientists began looking for ways to *cause* such changes in the laboratory. They were successful beyond their wildest dreams. British physicist Ernest Rutherford achieved the first of these successes in 1919 when he bombarded ordinary **nitrogen** gas with alpha particles. Rutherford found that an **isotope** (version) of **oxygen** gas, oxygen-17, was produced in the reaction. He had transmuted one element (nitrogen) into another element (oxygen).

Since then, scientists have explored almost every imaginable transmutation reaction. Subatomic particles such as **protons**, **neutrons**, and **electrons** have been used to bombard one element with the hope (usually realized) of producing a new and different element in the process.

One intriguing result of such research has been the creation of transuranium elements, elements with atomic numbers greater than 92 that do not exist in nature. When the very heaviest naturally occurring elements are bombarded with subatomic particles, or even with the nuclei of small atoms, new elements with atomic numbers as high as 109 have been created.

⋆⋆ Transplant, surgical

Transplants Throughout History

Stories of transplanted **tissue** and body parts go far back in myth and legend. It is said that in the sixth century A.D., the Christian patron saints of medicine, Cosmos and Damian, replaced the cancerous leg of a white man with the healthy leg of a recently deceased black man. In India as far back as the sixth century B.C., skin grafts were done to replace noses that had been amputated as a penalty for adultery.

This Indian practice was introduced to Western medicine by the Italian surgeon Gaspare Tagliacozzi in the sixteenth century. He attached a skin flap from a patient's forearm to the patient's nose. Several weeks later, he cut the flap (and the arm) from the nose. Tagliacozzi used the patient's own skin because he felt that foreign body tissue would be rejected. Thus he foresaw what is still the major problem with successful transplantation—rejection of foreign body tissue.

Skin grafting was reintroduced in the nineteenth century after French surgeon Jacques Louis Reverdin found in 1869 that successful grafts required thinner **tissue**. Scottish surgeon William MacEwen reported success with bone allografts (transplants from one person to another) in children in 1881. Most attempts at transplantation failed, however, because of inadequate surgical technique or rejection by the recipient.

In 1902 French surgeon Alexis Carrel developed a method of sewing together small blood vessels using tiny needles and fine thread. Testing this method with Charles Guthrie of the University of Chicago, Carrel performed a series of organ transplants on animals. While the transplants were

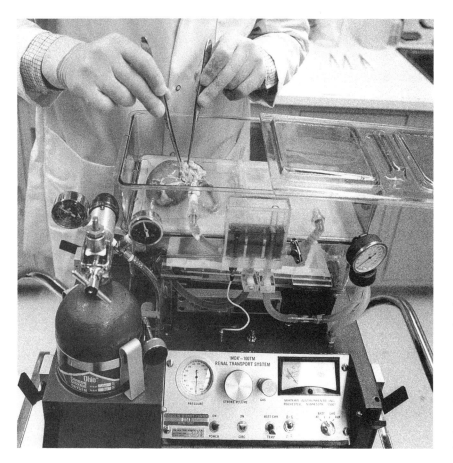

A kidney being prepared for transplant. The kidney was the first internal organ to be transplanted, in 1933, because of its relatively simple blood-supply system.

Heart Transplants Astound the World

South African physician Christiaan Barnard, drawing on techniques developed by Norman Shumway and Richard Lower of the United States, performed the first heart transplant in 1967. He took the heart of a young woman and implanted it in Louis Washansky, a 55-year-old grocer. Washansky survived only 18 days. Barnard's second patient, dentist Philip Blaiberg, lived for 17 months.

Heart transplantation became fairly routine. Denton Cooley of Houston, Texas, performed more than 20 in 1968. Outcomes, however, were very poor because immunosuppressants were not yet very effective. Heart transplantation virtually died out in the 1970s. Then, when cyclosporin came into wide use after 1983, heart transplants began again and were then successful.

at first successful—the organs functioned well for a while—they soon failed. Other experimenters had similar results and transplantation was at a standstill.

Studies in Rejection

Researchers experimenting with transplants began to suspect that the body's rejection of the implanted organ was an **immune system** response to foreign **tissue**. British biologist Peter Medawar became interested in skin graft problems while working with severely burned soldiers during World War II (1939-45). He found that a second set of skin grafts taken between the same two subjects was rejected twice as quickly as the first set. To Medawar, this was clearly an immune response. Further experiments revealed that grafts between twins were not rejected. Medawar went on to prove, in 1954, that immune tolerance was acquired during an embryo's development. Injection of foreign substances into embryonic or newborn mice would produce permanent tolerance to those substances later in life.

Meanwhile, surgeons continued to experiment with transplants, focusing their efforts on the kidney because of its relatively simple blood-supply system. Russian surgeon Yuri Voronoy performed the first human kidney transplant in Kiev, Ukraine, in 1933. Kidney transplants carried out in cities throughout the world all failed, although one patient, a 26-year-old Boston doctor, lived for six months with his new organ. Matching donor's and recipient's blood types did not improve outcomes either.

A Boston team finally achieved success in 1954. A 24-year-old man was dying of kidney disease. He was referred along with his twin brother to the Boston team. The transplant from twin to twin did succeed. The door was now open, and the Boston surgical team performed 23 identical-twin kidney transplants between 1954 and 1966. However, transplants between non-twins still resulted in rejection. Doctors remained unsuccessful at suppressing the immune response by **X-raying** the whole body and the organ to be transplanted.

Two major breakthroughs in the early 1960s finally addressed the rejection problem. Beginning in 1962, it became possible to match donor and recipient tissue closely. This technique markedly decreased the likelihood of rejection in transplantation. Then, two physicians showed that a drug called 6-mercaptopurine could suppress the immune response. They called this effect "immunosuppression." An improved immunosuppressant called Imuran (azathioprine) came into standard use in 1962, and kidney transplantation—with extended survival—became routine. Thomas Starzl of the University of Colorado developed the now-standard use of steroids along with azathioprine in 1963.

Immunosuppressant therapy was greatly improved by the discovery of cyclosporin in 1972. The widespread use of cyclosporin ushered in the era of widespread organ transplantation. Again, Starzl showed cyclosporin to be more effective when used with steroids.

Current State of Transplantation

The liver remains difficult to transplant because of its complicated blood supply. The first successful liver transplant was performed by Starzl at the University of Colorado in 1967. Cyclosporin greatly improved the outcome of these transplants.

The first human pancreas transplantation was first performed by Richard Lillehei and William Kelly of the University of Minnesota in 1966.

South African physician Christiaan Barnard performed the first heart transplant in 1967.

Because transplantation of both lungs succeeds better than transplanting a single lung, and because most patients with end-stage lung disease also have serious heart deterioration, heart-lung (heart and both lungs) transplants are sometimes performed. The success of this operation is aided by cyclosporin. The first successful operation of this type was carried out in 1981 at Stanford University Medical Center by Bruce Reitz and Norman Shumway.

Other body parts are now transplanted, but problems remain. Many grafts do not survive permanently. Cyclosporin is very expensive and has serious side effects. Graft-versus-host rejection, in which lymphocytes (a variety of white blood cells) in the transplanted tissue attack the "foreign" host tissue, is difficult to control. Still, a 1992 government report found that organ transplants in the United States were largely successful, with favorable outcome rates varying according to the organ transplanted.

⋆⋆ TRH
(thyrotropin-releasing hormone)

Thyrotropin-releasing **hormone** (TRH) is produced by the portion of the brain called the hypothalamus. It is the first in the series of hormones that stimulates the thyroid gland to produce thyroxine, which is used by the body to promote **protein** synthesis and growth.

When the **blood** registers a low level of thyroxine, the hypothalamus receives a message to produce TRH. This is transported to the part of the pituitary gland that produces thyroid-stimulating hormone (TSH, or thyrotropin). TSH is then transported to the thyroid gland, which produces thyroxine (also called T4) and another hormone, triiodothyronine (T3).

In 1968 TRH was the first hypothalamic hormone to be isolated and synthesized. This was done by the American endocrinologists (hormone doctors) Roger Guillemin and Andrew Victor Schally. The synthesized form of TRH was found to be active in all species of vertebrates (creatures with backbones) and soon was used to diagnose tumors of the pituitary gland and to measure pituitary function. For their work on this and other hormones, Guillemin and Schally received part of the 1977 Nobel Prize in physiology or medicine.

⋆⋆ Tungsten

Tungsten is a hard, brittle, corrosion-resistant (not prone to rust or decay), metallic element. Tungsten's greatest assets are its high melting point 6170°F (3410° C), which is higher than that of any other metal, and its ability to retain its strength at very high temperatures. These properties make tungsten (atomic number 74) extremely useful in the manufacture and use of many alloys, which are mixtures of metals.

The name "tungsten" comes from the Swedish tung sten, which means "heavy stone.

Discovery

In nature, tungsten is mainly found in the minerals scheelite and wolframite. In 1781 German-born Swedish chemist Carl Wilhelm Scheele examined scheelite (which is named after him) and found that a new acid could be produced from it. The acid Scheele prepared was tungstic acid.

In 1783 Spanish mineralogist Don Fausto d'Elhuyar and his older brother, Juan Jose d'Elhuyar, obtained tungstic acid from wolframite. Recognizing that this was the same acid that Scheele had produced just two years earlier, the d'Elhuyar brothers reduced the acid and discovered the new metal, tungsten. Because it was first obtained from wolframite, tungsten is also called "wolfram," and its chemical symbol is W.

Uses

In the late 1800s, scientists found that unlike most metals, which soften when heated, steel alloys made with tungsten would remain hard at very high temperatures. This discovery anticipated the start of today's high-speed tool industry. Being hard and tough, tungsten resists heat friction better. Since it is more durable than ordinary steel, tungsten is used to make tools that can operate at higher temperatures. Other tungsten alloys are used in automobile ignition systems, electric furnaces, vacuum tubes, and space missiles. Tungsten carbide, an extremely hard compound, is used in mining and oil drilling, while other tungsten compounds are used in fluorescent lamps. Tungsten's chief use is as a filament for electric light bulbs.

See also **Electromagnetism**

⋆⋆ Tunnel

Tunnels are underground passageways used for transportation, mining, drainage purposes, and for installation of power sources.

Early civilizations relied on tunnels to carry water for drinking and irrigation. The Egyptians tunneled into cliffs to construct temples. As far back as 2100 B.C., the Babylonians actually diverted (turned aside from its course) the Euphrates River long enough to build a pedestrian tunnel underneath it. The Greeks and Romans practiced tunneling extensively, the Romans constructing aqueduct (water-carrying) tunnels through mountains.

Tunnel technology went dormant until about the 1700s, when tunnels were included in the development of **canal** networks in Europe and North America. The use of gunpowder to blast through solid rock was a major advance. Different explosives are used today, but the blasting technique remains about the same.

A subway tunnel under construction. Tunnels are underground passageways used for transportation, mining, drainage purposes, and for installation of power sources.

As railroads were extensively developed beginning in the 1830s, tunnels became crucial elements of the rail system. Trains had to run on the lowest possible grade slope (as level as possible), so tunnels were built in tremendous numbers.

Techniques

Cave-ins that occurred during the building of the Thames River Tunnel led to the 1825 development of a cast-iron tunneling shield for the pro-

tection of workers. Peter Barlow improved the shield in 1869, and James Greathead used compressed air to reduce seepage of water and mud into the work space. Compressed air was also used in construction of the London subway in 1886.

While hand-drilling was standard practice before the Hoosac Tunnel—the first U.S. railroad tunnel—was begun in 1855, **dynamite** and compressed-air drills were used for the first time during its construction.

The twentieth century has seen the development of several tunneling machines. The rotary excavator, or mole, forces its way forward through the bedrock. The loosened rock is then carried back through the tunnel in "muck cars."

Rock mechanics has become a major part of tunnel planning, since a number of disasters have occurred because the rock structure was either not evaluated or was misjudged. Therefore, the mass of the rock is now analyzed and geological stress predicted, since stress from earthquakes and other past geologic events can affect the tunnel.

Another important consideration in tunnel construction is stand-up time—the amount of time, whether seconds or hours, that an excavated

Mining shafts such as this and tunnel networks can extend miles into the earth.

Tunneling is difficult and dangerous but the benefits are worth the effort.

Famous Tunnels

In the early 1800s, the father-and-son team of Marc Isambard Brunel and Isambard K. Brunel engineered the Thames River Tunnel, the world's first underwater tunnel, in London, England.

In 1855 the 412-mile (662.908 km) Hoosac Tunnel, begun in the Berkshire Mountains of Massachusetts, became the first railroad tunnel in the United States. It took 18 years to complete, but many new procedures were developed in the process.

Construction on the English Channel Tunnel, an engineer's dream for centuries, began in 1987. Referred to locally as "The Chunnel," it is the first physical link between Britain and the European Continent. The initial breakthrough, or pilot bore, was made in 1991. Completed in 1993, the 31-mile (48.27 km) tunnel accommodates special trains that ferry automobiles by flatcar. A second highway tunnel is proposed to begin in the year 2000.

Other such monumental tunneling projects will likely be attempted. It may be more realistic to consider a tunnel or submerged conduit for the Strait of Gibraltar, for example, than to attempt to bridge it. The Strait of Gibraltar separates Spain from the northern tip of Africa.

stretch will stand without support. The tunneling crew has to reinforce the tunnel at its heading or excavation face.

Most modern tunnels have been built to accommodate **automobile** traffic. Many major automobile tunnels run under rivers and harbors, and trench tunnels are preferred for these situations. In this method a trench is dug at the bottom of the body of water. Then the tunnel sections, often double-barreled for opposite traffic flow, are lowered into the trench, buried and drained of water.

Pipe-jacking is used for smaller tunnels. This involves lowering pipe segments into a vertical shaft, then moving them into place as the tunnel boring (widening) progresses.

Mining shafts and tunnel networks can extend miles into the earth, both vertically and horizontally. Despite all precautions, underground mining is quite dangerous. Gases can accumulate in pockets of a mine, causing explosions. The noise from the machinery can damage hearing and make communication difficult. Finally, cave-ins are a constant threat.

See also **Train and railroad**

⋆⋆ Tunneling

During the 1920s, the French physicist Louis de Broglie introduced the notion that particles can have wave properties. The equations that he, Erwin Schrödinger, and other physicists developed to describe these properties led to some startling new interpretations of particle behavior. One of these properties has come to be known as "tunneling."

In classical physics, a charged particle is not allowed to pass through certain regions where the energy is too high for it to overcome. Quantum mechanical wave theory offers a somewhat different perspective on this phenomenon. It says that the particle has some small, but non-zero, chance of passing through that energy barrier provided that the barrier is thin enough. The name given to the phenomenon suggests that the particle may "tunnel under" the apparently insurmountable energy barrier.

No opportunity to test this prediction was available before the 1950s. Then, research on semiconductors resulted in the development of materials in which tunneling can be observed. The first convincing evidence for tunneling was obtained by Japanese physicist Leo Esaki in 1957. Esaki constructed a pn diode (an electronic device through which current can pass only in one direction) in which both semiconductors were heavily doped. The doping resulted in an abundance of electrons in the n semiconductor and an abundance of holes in the p semiconductor. Esaki then connected the two semiconductors by means of a very thin insulating film. He found that a current flowed across the apparently resistant barrier, providing evidence of the occurrence of tunneling.

The next step in tunneling research came about in 1960 when Norwegian physicist Ivar Giaever examined the nature of tunneling in superconducting materials. By carefully selecting the metals used in the diode and the temperatures at which they were maintained, Giaever was able to determine fundamental properties of the superconducting elements. One consequence of his research was the collection of evidence to support the recently announced BCS theory of **superconductivity**, which explains the resistantless flow of electrons characteristic of a superconductor.

The Nobel Prize for physics was awarded in 1973 to Esaki, Giaever, and Brian Josephson for their work on tunneling. Josephson's contribution to that effort came in 1962 when he was still a graduate student. Josephson's study of tunneling led him to predict two kinds of effects, one that would be observed with AC current, and the other with DC current. In the former (AC) case, Josephson predicted the appearance of an oscillating (wavering) current between the two elements of the diode that would have a frequency of 483.6 megahertz per microvolt drop across the gap. In the latter (DC) case, Josephson predicted that a current would flow across the gap between two superconductors, even if there were no voltage drop across the gap. The two predicted phenomena were soon observed by American physicists.

The work of Esaki, Giaever, and Josephson led to a vastly improved understanding of the fundamental structure of matter. It also has been used in the development of a variety of instruments used in research and industry. Highly sensitive devices known as superconducting quantum interference devices (SQUIDS), for example, are now widely used in instruments such as magnetometers, voltmeters, low-temperature thermometers, and high-speed computers.

⋆⋆ Tupperware

Earl Tupper's products were made of a new lighter weight yet stronger plastic he developed while working at Du Pont.

Tupperware includes everything from eating utensils—bowls, tumblers, and serving pieces—to children's toys, all made from a sturdy **plastic** material. It was invented by Earl Tupper in the 1930s.

Tupper, an American molding engineer who once worked for Du Pont, developed a synthetic **polymer** that produced a pliable but sturdy plastic. He called his creation "Poly T" and began to manufacture various household items from the new material. Among the items were poker chips and ice cube trays. His products competed strongly with other plastic items available at the time, which were heavy and easily broken. His new plastic was not affected by anything except knife cuts and boiling water.

While still at Du Pont, Tupper started a successful mail-order business and was able to strike out on his own in 1937. He founded the Tupperware Corporation in 1942. World War II (1939-45) interrupted the production of the corporation's first product, a 7-ounce (207ml) bathroom tumbler, which finally appeared in 1945. The following year the product was reissued in decorator pastel shades.

By 1947 the company introduced what is probably its most famous product—nesting plastic bowls with airtight lids. The popular bowls initially sold for about 39 cents each. Before then, the only unbreakable eating utensils had been made from aluminum. Tupper's new plastic products were praised for both their household and institutional uses. The Museum of Modern Art in New York City even asked for one of the bowls for a display of useful objects. Sales in 1947 totaled $5 million.

By the 1950s, Tupper had discovered that his products sold best through in-home sales parties. His Tupperware Home Parties involved games, refreshments, and Tupperware demonstrations. During the next three years, 9,000 dealers came on board, and sales soared to $25 million. Retail sales (in stores) of the product were then discontinued.

Tupperware Corporation was sold to Rexall Drugs in 1958 for more than $9 million. Premark International of Deerfield, Illinois, currently owns Tupperware Home Parties, which enjoyed net sales of more than $1 billion in 1990. Tupper died in 1983.

⋆⋆ Typewriter

The typewriter is a machine that prints characters and numerals one after the other on a sheet of paper when keys are pressed. Attempts to design such a machine began in the eighteenth century, mainly with the intention of creating raised characters for reading by the blind. The first recorded patent for a typewriter was issued by Queen Anne of England in January 1714. Its inventor, engineer Henry Mill, described "An Artificial Machine or Method for the Impressing or Transcribing of Letters Singly or Progressively one after the other." No drawing or model of the device exists.

The first United States patent for a "typographer" was issued in 1829 to William A. Burt of Detroit, Michigan. The letters on his table-size printer were set around a circular carriage, which was rotated by hand—a very slow process. An improved circular-carriage machine was patented by Charles Thurber in 1845. It rotated automatically and featured an inked roller.

The ancestor of the type-bar machine was invented by Xavier Projean, a French printer. His *machine cryptographique* had each character mounted on a single, separate bar. Projean proudly claimed that his machine would write almost as fast as a **pen**.

QWERTY

The commercial typewriter we know today owes much to the work

The typewriter brought about profound social change as women discovered they could earn a living using it.

Typewriter

of Christopher Latham Sholes, an American printer and editor, and Carlos Glidden and Samuel W. Soulé. Sholes and Soulé had been working to develop a machine to print book page numbers when Glidden suggested designing the machine to print letters of the alphabet as well. Glidden also pointed out to Sholes a *Scientific American* article about a typewriting machine recently invented by John Pratt of London.

The commercial typewriter we know today owes much to the work of American printer and editor Christopher Sholes.

With help from Glidden and Soulé, Sholes designed a type-bar machine with a carriage that automatically moved one space to the left when a letter was printed. He rearranged the keyboard from an alphabetical arrangement that caused the bars of the machine to jam. In his new arrangement, the most-used letters were arranged apart from each other so that jamming would not occur when fast typing was being done. The system is known as QWERTY because those are the first six letters on the keyboard.

In 1873 Sholes interested the Remington Fire Arms company in the machine. Remington was looking for new products other than weapons, because the arms manufacturing business had collapsed following the end of the Civil War (1861-65). The company bought Sholes's patents for $12,000 and put the Remington Model 1 on the market in 1876. One of the first was purchased by American writer Mark Twain (1835-1910), who used it to produce the first typed manuscript for a publisher.

The typewriter did not catch on immediately. Remington gave up on it, selling the rights to it in 1886. By the early 1890s, however, business offices had discovered the machine. The mass market in typewriters boomed, and with it came profound social change. Women by the millions found a new, respectable form of employment using a typewriter.

One of the first typewriters was purchased by Mark Twain, who used it to produce the first typed manuscript for a publisher.

Many improvements were made to the early Remington model. A shift-key mechanism was added in 1878 so lowercase as well as capital letters could be typed. Double keyboards, featuring separate keys for capital and small letters, also appeared, but they did not work well and eventually disappeared. American inventor John Williams developed the front-stroke machine in 1890. With it, characters could be seen as they were being produced. The first portable typewriter, the Blick, was available in the early 1890s.

Twentieth-Century Innovations

Electricity was added to the typewriter in the 1920s, bringing about a more even, effortless, and faster operation. Portable electric typewriters were introduced in 1956. IBM came out with its spherical type element (the round font) and stationary (it did not move) paper carriage in 1961. Typewriters with correction tape appeared on the market in 1973, and rotating print wheels were added in 1978. IBM introduced the first electric typewriter with a memory in 1965. Voice-activated typewriters are under development. Advances in electronics and microprocessors allow today's typewriters to function like personal computers for many types of word processing.

⋆⋆⋆ Typing correction fluid

By 1968 Liquid Paper was producing more than 10,000 bottles per day and sales totaled $1 million.

In the old days, people used **typewriters** with a carbon film ribbon. If a person made an error and tried to use an **eraser** to correct it, a smudged black splotch was left on the paper.

Bette Nesmith Graham, born Bette Claire McMurray in 1924 in Dallas, Texas, was working as an executive secretary at Texas Bank & Trust in Dallas in 1951. Graham reasoned that she should be able to cover her typing mistakes with white, tempera waterbase paint, also known as poster paint. She began bringing a small bottle of this liquid and a brush to work with her. Her coworkers requested bottles of their own, and by 1956 she had a thriving business with her son Michael. Together they filled more than 100 bottles a month of "Mistake Out" in their garage. Graham decided it was time to patent her product and trademark the name, which she changed to Liquid Paper. An article about her invention appeared in a national magazine and orders increased.

By 1968 Liquid Paper was producing more than 10,000 bottles a day and sales totaled $1 million. By the middle of the 1970s, the company was producing 25 million bottles a year, and in 1979 the Gillette Corporation bought Liquid Paper for more than $47 million.

Graham died in 1980. She left half of her $50 million estate to her favorite charities and the other half to her son, Michael Nesmith. Michael made a name for himself in the 1970s as a member of the musical group The Monkees.

⋆ Ultrasonic wave

Ultrasonic waves are sound waves pitched too high for human ears to detect. Their frequencies range from 20,000 hertz (about the top range for the human ear) to about ten trillion hertz. A hertz is a unit of frequency equal to one cycle per second.

Ultrasonic waves are pressure waves with the ability to both shake and penetrate many materials. Pressure waves are also called compression waves. They are created when a very dense material vibrates very fast. This causes the air around the material to be alternately pushed and pulled, producing regular pressure variations. At very high frequencies, such as the ultrasonic range, the compression wave can be focused into a fine "beam" which can then be used to vibrate particles in its path. To generate an ultrasonic beam, you must use a transducer—a device that converts electrical or magnetic energy into kinetic, or mechanical, energy.

Many animals, such as dogs and bats, can hear sounds that are pitched too high for humans to detect. They are hearing ultrasonic sound waves.

Applications in Research, Industry, Medicine

There are numerous practical applications for ultrasonics. The first widespread use was in underwater exploration. Ultrasonic waves proved to be an excellent method for determining the depth of water. Ultrasonics are used to map the topography (surface) of lake and ocean floors. During World War II (1939-45), submarines used ultrasonic waves to maintain secret contact with each other.

In industry, ultrasonic waves have been used in the testing of machinery and machine parts. Using a narrow beam of sound, engineers can look inside metal parts in much the same way doctors use **X-rays** to examine the human body. With ultrasonic technology, flaws in machinery can be detected and repaired before they cause damage.

Similar ultrasonic diagnostic methods have been developed for use on the human body. In medicine this method is called "ultrasound." As an ultrasonic beam passes through the human body, it encounters different types of **tissue** such as flesh, bone, and organs. Each type of tissue causes the beam to reflect in a different way. By studying these reflections, physicians can accurately map the interior of the body. Unlike X-rays, there is no risk of harmful overexposure with ultrasonics. So they have become a useful alternative to X-rays, and are often used on sensitive organs, such as kidneys, as well as to monitor the progress of pregnancies.

Because they can vibrate the particles they pass through, ultrasonic waves are often used to shake, or even destroy, certain materials. A good example of this is ultrasonic emulsification. In this technique, two liquids that do not normally mix (such as oil and water) are made to vibrate until they are blended. This technique is also used to remove air bubbles from molten metals before casting so that the finished piece will be free of cavities. Doctors also use it to break up kidney and gall stones, thus avoiding surgery.

Ultrasonic vibration can also be used to kill **bacteria** in milk and other liquids. Some inventors are attempting to perfect an "ultrasonic laundry," using high-frequency vibrations to shake dirt and other particles out of clothing.

See also **Electromagnetism; Magnetic field; Ultrasound device; Wave motion, law of**

⋆⋆ Ultrasound device

Before the development of ultrasound devices, there was no way to diagnose the condition of a fetus without **prenatal surgery**—a procedure that was extremely risky for both the mother and the unborn child. Another method was the use of X-ray radiation, but it soon became apparent that prolonged exposure to X-rays was hazardous, especially to a fetus. In fact, a 1958 study showed that there was a much higher rate of leukemia (a blood disease in which there are too many white blood cells) among children exposed to radiation *in utero* (in the womb).

The same year that study appeared, however, a new science was introduced—the science of ultrasonography. Using high-frequency sound waves, physicians were able to observe the condition of an unborn child without apparent danger to the child or the mother.

British Develop Technology

The man most responsible for the development of ultrasound technology was the British physician Ian Donald. During World War II (1939-45), Donald was serving in the British Royal Air Force, while experiments were being conducted on **radar** and **sonar** devices. This technology was then classified as top secret, but it was released to the scientific community following the end of the war—about the same time Donald began his medical career.

Ultrasonics was first used to test machine parts, to detect cracks, flaws, and bubbles in the metal. Donald was certain that ultrasonics could

Through the use of ultrasound, physicians are able to observe the condition of an unborn child without apparent danger to the child or the mother.

How Ultrasonics Works

Ultrasonics works because sound waves of very high frequencies can easily and harmlessly penetrate human flesh. As the waves enter the body, they encounter substances of different densities, such as bone and internal organs. These various thicknesses bounce back the waves differently to the wave source. Because each substance makes the waves reflect differently, physicians can identify the type of **tissue** by the type of reflection. An ultrasound machine uses the different signals to create a picture of the inside of the body.

Because of the safety of the procedure, ultrasonics has been applied to the diagnosis of other delicate organs such as the heart, lungs, and kidneys.

be applied in medicine, particularly in his field of obstetrics (the care of women during pregnancy). In the early 1950s, he began working with engineers to modify the devices to observe the human body.

Donald's ultrasonic device for medical diagnosis was first tested in 1957. With it, Donald used sound waves to correctly diagnose a patient's heart condition. A year later the procedure called ultrasonography was being used on pregnant women.

Since the 1960s, improvements to ultrasonographic technology have made it the most common procedure for observing the fetus. The information gained helps obstetricians in treating individual pregnancies. In the thousands of ultrasonographs performed, no evidence of harmful effects has been found. Because of the safety of the procedure, ultrasonics has been applied to the diagnosis of other delicate organs such as the heart, lungs, and kidneys.

Treats Certain Ailments

Ultrasonics is now being used in the treatment of certain conditions as well as for observation. A device called the Cavitron was invented in 1980. It focuses a narrow beam of sound waves on a tumor, breaking it up without removing it from the body. A similar method is used to pulverize (break into pieces) gall stones, making their passage much less painful. (Gall stones are small, hard objects that form in the gall bladder.)

The Cavitron is an effective tool for treating ailments that previously required invasive surgery. It is particularly useful in the treatment of brain tumors.

See also **Submarine; X-ray machine**

. Ultraviolet astronomy

Optical telescopes, the kind we are probably most familiar with, use mirrors and lenses to gather light for magnification. They have been in use for 400 years. But visible light is a small part of the overall spectrum of **electromagnetic waves**. Beyond the violet portion of visible light are high-energy ultraviolet rays, **X-rays** and cosmic rays. Each wavelength gives a different "picture" of the sky.

Because very hot stars produce more energy in the ultraviolet wavelengths than in visible light, what astronomers see with their eyes is just a small part of the star's total energy output. To get a better understanding of the star's energy, scientists must be able to "see" other wavelengths, as well. "Seeing" **ultraviolet radiation** poses some special problems.

Earth's **ozone** layer, for instance, absorbs this type of high-energy radiation. The only way to detect ultraviolet radiation is by satellite. The first opportunity to "see" such radiation presented itself after World War II (1939-45). Several captured German V-2 rockets were launched with ultraviolet detectors (spectrometers) on board. These special "eyes" discovered far-ultraviolet radiation coming from the **Sun**.

Once the space age got underway in the 1950s, there were many more opportunities to study the ultraviolet sky. By the 1970s, ultraviolet telescopes (which work much the same way as optical telescopes except for the addition of a special coating on the optics) were placed aboard *Skylab,* America's only scientific space station to carry astronauts.

A series of eight Orbiting Solar Observatories (OSOs) were launched by the National Aeronautics and Space Administration (NASA) from 1962 through 1975. They carried instruments to observe ultraviolet radiation from specific regions of the sun. These satellites greatly increased astronomers' knowledge about the structure of the solar corona.

NASA launched two Orbiting Astronomical Observatories (OAOs) between 1968 and 1972. They were designed to look deep into space beyond our **solar system**. The second launch, OAO *Copernicus,* discovered a great deal about the make-up, temperature, and structure of interstellar (space) gas. The most successful ultraviolet satellite, launched in 1978, was the *International Ultraviolet Explorer* (*IUE*). This satellite was expected to last only three years, but astronauts celebrated its tenth anniversary by focusing *IUE* on the exploding star *Supernova 1987A.*

Ultraviolet telescopes have helped us learn about how stars are formed and about what lies between them in the vast reaches of space.

Before the launch of ultraviolet observatories, scientists believed that what lay between the stars was cool **hydrogen**. However, the satellites discovered extensive regions of ionized interstellar gas surrounding the hotter luminous stars. These areas, called Hydrogen II (H II) regions, are responsible for emission and reflection nebulas. The best example of an emission nebula is the Orion Nebula. This nebula is believed to be a stellar nursery, an area where stars are in the process of forming. The H II region around the stars of the Pleiades cluster is an example of a reflection nebula.

Ultraviolet astronomy has contributed a great deal to our understanding of the evolution and formation of the stars.

⋆⋆ Ultraviolet radiation

Ultraviolet light causes tanning and sunburns, and overexposure to it can lead to skin cancer.

Just like visible light, infrared light, and radio waves, ultraviolet light is electromagnetic radiation. On the spectrum, ultraviolet light lies between violet light and **X-rays**, with wavelengths ranging from 4 to 4,000 nanometers (one-billionth of a meter). Although it is invisible to the naked eye, anyone who has been exposed to too much sunlight has probably noted the effects of ultraviolet light. This is the radiation that causes tanning and sunburns and can lead to skin cancer.

Discovery

The man credited with the discovery of ultraviolet light is the German physicist Johann Ritter. Ritter had been experimenting with silver chloride, a chemical known to break down when exposed to sunlight. He found that the light at the blue end of the visible spectrum—blue, indigo, violet—was a much more efficient catalyst for this reaction. Experimenting further, he discovered that silver chloride broke down most efficiently when exposed to radiation just beyond the blues—radiation that was invisible to the eye. He called this new type of radiation "ultraviolet," meaning "beyond the violet."

Ultraviolet Lamps

Three varieties of ultraviolet lamps produce ultraviolet light of a different intensity. Near-ultraviolet lamps are fluorescent lights whose visible light has been blocked, releasing ultraviolet radiation just beyond the visible spectrum. These lamps are also known as black lights, and are used mainly to make fluorescent paints and dyes "glow" in the dark. This effect is often seen in the entertainment industry, but can also be used by industry to detect flaws in machine parts.

Middle-ultraviolet lamps produce radiation of a slightly shorter wavelength. They generally use a stimulated arc of **mercury** vapor and a specially designed glass bulb. Because middle-ultraviolet radiation is very similar to that produced by the **Sun**, these lamps are frequently used as sunlamps and are often found in tanning salons and greenhouses. Photochemical lamps that generate middle-ultraviolet light are also used in industry, as well as by chemists to induce certain chemical reactions.

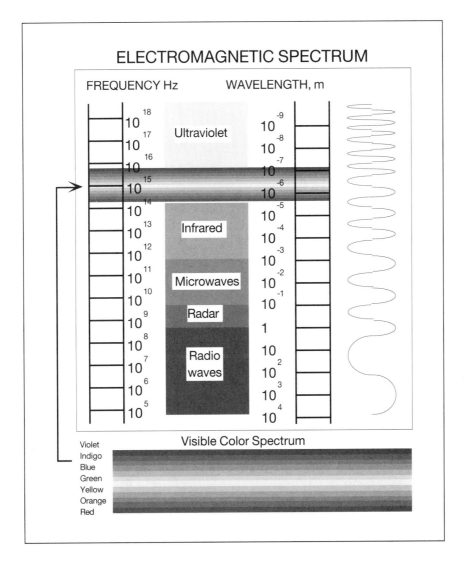

The electromagnetic spectrum and the visible color spectrum. Ultraviolet light is electromagnetic radiation. On the electromagnetic spectrum, ultraviolet light lies between violet light and X-rays.

Body's Use of UV Radiation

While ultraviolet (UV) radiation in large doses is hazardous to humans, a certain amount is required by the body. As it strikes the skin it activates the chemical processes that produce vitamin D. In areas where there is not enough sunshine, children often suffer from a disease called rickets. In order to treat this disease or to supplement natural light in sun-starved communities, ultraviolet lamps that provide vitamin D are often used in place of natural sources.

Far-ultraviolet lamps produce high-energy, short-wavelength ultraviolet light. Like middle-ultraviolet lamps, they use mercury-vapor tubes. However, far-ultraviolet radiation is easily absorbed by glass, and so the lamp's bulb must be constructed from quartz. Far-ultraviolet light has been found to destroy living organisms such as germs and **bacteria**. For this reason, these lamps are used to sterilize hospital air and equipment. Far-ultraviolet radiation has also been used to kill bacteria in food and milk, giving perishables a much longer shelf life.

Astronomical Uses

A more passive application of ultraviolet light is in astronomy. Much of the light emitted by stars, particularly very young stars, is in the ultraviolet range. By observing the output of ultraviolet light, astronomers can determine the temperature and composition of stars and interstellar gas, as well as gain insights into the evolution of galaxies. However, most of the ultraviolet light from distant sources is unable to penetrate Earth's atmosphere. Therefore, ultraviolet observations must be made from Earth orbit, by sounding rockets, **space probes,** or astronomical satellites.

See also **Electromagnetism; Fluorescence and phosphorescence; Photochemistry**

⋆⋆ Umbrella

A collapsible device forming a canopy to protect the bearer from the sun or rain has been in use for more than 3,000 years. In many countries such a device has been used as a ceremonial item and to show high rank.

The umbrella is known to have been in use in China in the eleventh century B.C. It was reportedly invented by a woman. Members of the Chinese royal family and other aristocrats used an umbrella carried by a servant who trailed several steps behind. The umbrella is also known to have existed in ancient Egypt. In ancient Greece and Rome, umbrellas were carried only by women—men who carried them were laughed at.

The umbrella was introduced to the rest of Europe by the Greeks about 2,000 years ago. In the sixteenth century, the Roman Catholic Pope declared the umbrella a symbol of honor and was seen under one whenever he appeared in public. By the middle of the eighteenth century, Englishmen began to use them daily as protection from frequent rain showers, although its first British enthusiast, Jonas Hanway, was teased mercilessly. In fact, cab drivers, who saw the umbrella as a threat to their business, would purposely spray mud and shout insults at Hanway.

By the nineteenth century Americans were using them too. The parasol (from the French words for "to shield" and "sun") was seen in Paris and London. Elegant ladies carried parasols decorated with fringe, lace and beads. An umbrella, hat, and gloves had become the mark of a well-dressed gentleman by the middle of the twentieth century.

The first umbrella frames were usually made of wood and were heavy and clumsy. Whalebone became the next material of choice, and by 1850 steel was used. Umbrella covers were made of silk, linen, and alpaca (the silky wool of a South American mammal). Modern umbrellas use a lightweight metal or **plastic** frame with a **nylon** or **polyester** cover. Some of them fold into such a small bundle that they can be tucked into a purse or pocket.

*"Umbrella"
comes from the
Latin word
umbra, which
means shade.
The Italian
word ombrella
means "little
shade."*

⋆*⋆ Underwater photography

British engineer and amateur photographer William Thompson devised the first method of taking underwater photographs in 1856. As he watched a swollen river sweep beneath a bridge during a rainstorm, he wondered whether the bridge would collapse. Next he wondered whether divers carrying cameras could help assess the damage.

To find out, Thompson and a friend placed a camera inside a watertight container and covered one end of the box with plate glass. Over the glass they put a wooden shutter, which could be raised and lowered by a string. They focused the lens and loaded a dry photographic plate into the camera. Thompson then rowed into Weymouth Bay and lowered the device to a depth of 18 feet (5.5 m). He pulled the shutter, and left his creation underwater for ten minutes. Unfortunately, the container yielded to pressure, and the camera filled with water. Thompson did obtain a faint image of the bay bottom, and submitted it to the Society of Arts in London as the first underwater photograph.

In 1893 Louis Boutan, a French professor of zoology, developed the forerunner of the underwater camera and a magnesium flash bulb, which was later replaced by more sophisticated underwater lighting methods.

American scientist Charles William Beebe took the first underwater photographs at extreme depths in 1935. He descended nearly 3,000 feet (900 m) in a bathyscaphe—a submersible ship with a watertight cabin used in deep-sea exploration. Ten years later American geophysicist Maurice Ewing devised the first automatic underwater camera to photograph deep-water geological structures.

See also **Photography**

⋆⋆ Uniformitarianism

Uniformitarianism is one theory about how the world was created. It states that Earth's physical structure is the result of currently existing forces that have operated uniformly (in the same way) since Earth began.

Early theories of Earth's formation were based on a literal reading of the Biblical book of Genesis. That is, people believed the Genesis story of the seven day creation period meant exactly what it said. So, using that reading, Earth could only be 6,000 years old.

James Hutton's Theory

In 1785 James Hutton, a Scottish geologist, presented to the Royal Society of Edinburgh (Scotland) a paper called *System of the Earth*. Hutton's paper contained the major elements of what was later termed "uniformitarianism." In it, he presented evidence that contradicted the Bible-based reading. Hutton maintained that:

- The fossilized strata (levels) of the earth, originating from the bottom of the sea, were formed by natural processes driven by heat energy from **Earth's core**.

- The present continents' shapes indicated that they had once belonged to a singular landmass. Hutton added that the current disintegration and erosion of surface rock would lead to the formation of future continents.

- These earth-shaping processes were natural and operated very slowly, and most of this activity predated humankind by much more than a few days.

Hutton's theory at first electrified the geologic community but later became the standard of modern geology.

Although Hutton did not live to see the profound effect of his theory on the geologic community, uniformitarianism gained momentum after his ideas were published by John Playfair. Playfair elaborated on Hutton's ideas in the influential *Illustrations of the Huttonian Theory* (1802). About 30 years later, the first great geological textbook, *Principles of Geology,* was written by Sir Charles Lyell, an English geologist. Using illustrations and examples from around the world, he explained the principle of uniformity so persuasively that it became the authoritative geological reference book in the Western world.

See also **Continental drift; Evolutionary theory**

⋆ Uranium

Uranium is a heavy, silvery-white metallic element found in several minerals, including pitchblende. It was probably used as far back as A.D. 79. Green glass taken from a Roman mural and found to date back to that period contained about 1 percent uranium oxide. Archaeologists believe that the uranium oxide was intentionally added to color the glass.

Ancient technicians certainly had no understanding of the chemical nature of the material they were working with. In fact, the existence of uranium and its compounds (mixtures) was not acknowledged until 1789 when German chemist Martin Heinrich Klaproth analyzed pitchblende and obtained an unfamiliar yellow powder. He theorized that it contained a new element, which he named "uranium" in honor of the newly discovered planet, **Uranus.**

Uranium was of relatively little interest until 1896, when French physicist Antoine-Henri Becquerel discovered that pitchblende emitted a

Uranium, an essential ingredient in nuclear fuels and weapons, has changed the face of modern civilization.

form of radiation similar to that of **X-rays**. Further research showed that the **radioactivity** was produced by uranium and related elements in the pitchblende. The discovery opened a new era in chemistry and physics that transformed not only the sciences but the whole of human society as well.

Composition and Uses

Uranium's atomic number is 92, its atomic weight, 238.0289, and its chemical symbol, U. The element has a melting point of 2,070° F (1,132.3° C) and a boiling point of 6,904° F (3,818° C). Three naturally occurring **isotopes** (versions) of the element exist. Of these, uranium-238 is by far the most abundant, followed by uranium-235, and uranium-234 (0.0056 percent). Another 11 isotopes, all radioactive, have been produced artificially.

The discovery of **nuclear fission** in the late 1930s revealed a special property of the uranium-235 isotope. When bombarded with **neutrons**, the atomic nucleus of uranium-235 splits into two roughly equal parts and releases large amounts of energy and additional neutrons. This energy has been used to create electricity, to diagnose and treat illnesses, and in bombs and missiles. Uranium is also used as toners in photography, in the dyeing of silk and wool, in color glazes, and in the leather industry.

⋆⋆ Uranus

When Uranus was discovered in 1781, it was observed to be so far from the Sun (about 1.7 million miles) that it doubled the diameter of the solar system as it was then known.

Uranus is one of the four giant Jovian (Jupiter-like) planets, composed of light elements such as **hydrogen** and **helium** with very little rock content.

Ancient peoples could look up and see five planets in the sky: **Mercury**, **Venus**, **Mars**, **Jupiter**, and **Saturn**. These planets appeared to wander around in relationship to the "fixed" stars (the term "planet" means "wanderer"). For centuries, astronomers believed that just those five planets and Earth made up the scope of our **solar system**.

Discovery

Uranus is large enough to be visible with the naked eye but was mistaken for a star. Records indicate that the first Astronomer Royal for England, John Flamsteed, had cataloged it as a star in 1690.

In 1781, nearly 100 years later, Uranus was recognized as a planet. Credit for this discovery goes to William Herschel, a German musician who moved to England, developed a love for astronomy, and made his own high-quality telescopes. Herschel, with the aid of a catalog that listed all the stars then known, decided to calculate how far they were from Earth. While searching the constellation Gemini, he spotted a faint object that appeared to be a clear disk.

The next night Herschel found that the object had moved in relation to the stars near it and decided it might be a comet. He sent a letter telling of his discovery to two leading British astronomers. However, neither of the two men could verify his findings because Herschel's telescope was far superior to theirs.

Soon after, Swedish astronomer Anders Johan Lexell plotted the orbit of the new object and found that it was not a comet heading for the Sun. Instead, it was a new planet moving in a near circular orbit 19 astronomical units (a.u.) from the Sun (the distance from Earth to the Sun equals one a.u.). Although Herschel wanted to name the planet after the king of England, it became known as Uranus, in mythology the father of Saturn.

Herschel continued to observe the new planet. He found two moons revolving around Uranus: Titania and Oberon. In 1851 two more moons, Ariel and Umbria, were discovered. A fifth moon, Miranda, was discovered in 1948. All the moons are named for characters in plays by William Shakespeare.

Unique Orbit

Uranus had a surprise in store for observers of its moons. Usually the satellites (or moons) of planets orbit in the same plane as the planets do when they revolve around the Sun. However, the satellites of Uranus had orbital planes nearly vertical to the orbital plane of Uranus. This puzzled astronomers until someone suggested Uranus might be tipped over on its side. If this were true, then the planet was going around the Sun with its axis in the plane of its orbit, unlike every other planet, whose axes are generally upright on their orbits. Thus, the satellites of Uranus were orbiting around the planet's equator as do all other planets, but the planet itself was traveling around the Sun on its side.

William Herschel, a German musician with a love for astronomy, was the first to recognize that Uranus is a planet.

Serious thought went into trying to account for this phenomenon. The current theory says Uranus was hit by a huge moon-size body long ago, and the resulting debris (de-bree) eventually formed the satellites circling the planet.

Uranus was frustrating to observers. It did not have the clear markings of its two neighbors, Jupiter and Saturn. It did not have the spectacular rings of Saturn. It did have a bland, pale green face. And it was not until 1986 that its orbit could be determined, when the satellite *Voyager* flew by.

The satellites of Uranus orbit around the planet's equator as do all other planets, but the planet itself travels around the Sun on its side.

What *Voyager* Saw

The face of Uranus was so featureless that *Voyager*'s cameras revealed little to curious astronomers on Earth. Other instruments were more successful. Uranus's rotation was established at 17.24 hours (the speed accounts for the flattened appearance of the planet). Winds were clocked at over 400 miles per hour (643 kph). *Voyager*'s data also indicated that beneath Uranus's hydrogen and helium atmosphere is a vast "ocean" of water, **methane**, and ammonia that surrounds a molten core of heavy materials.

Voyager looked closely at the planet's faint ring system. These rings are extremely dark and narrow. The spacecraft discovered ten new moons apparently made of frozen water and rock. The moons were photographed and revealed grooved and cracked surfaces probably caused by tidal forces. Scientists assert that the *Voyager* exploration yielded more information about Uranus than all the knowledge that had been accumulated since the planet's discovery.

⋆⭑⋆ Urea

Urea is a white crystalline compound excreted in urine by humans and most other mammals. Urea is formed by the liver, primarily from the ammonia that results when excess **amino acids** are deaminized (or broken down).

Urea was first discovered in urine by the French chemist Jean Rouelle in 1773. It was synthesized in 1828 by German chemist Friedrich Wöhler. This was a feat more remarkable than it may sound.

Synthesis

In the early 1800s, it was widely believed that an organic compound such as urea, a product formed by the human body, could not be manufactured in the laboratory. When Wöhler found he had accidentally synthesized crystals of urea while evaporating a solution of ammonium cyanate, he was as surprised as any other chemist would be. In his excitement, he dashed off a letter to his friend, Swedish chemist Jöns Berzelius, declaring, "I can make urea without needing a kidney, whether of man or dog!"

Wöhler's historic accomplishment, the preparation of "artificial" urea, demonstrated to the scientific world that an organic compound could be synthesized by a chemist. For many, then, Wöhler is considered the true father of organic chemistry.

✲ Vacuum bottle

Today thousands of American school children carry a thermos of milk with their lunch. These thermoses are descendents of the vacuum bottle, invented in 1872. Invention of the vacuum bottle is credited to Scottish chemist and physicist James Dewar, who is best known for his work with the liquefaction (the process of making liquid) of gases at extremely low temperatures. His biggest hurdle was keeping the gases cool enough so they would remain liquid during storage.

In 1872 Dewar hit upon the idea of insulating a flask from the surrounding air by enclosing it in a larger flask and creating a vacuum (an empty space) between the two. The vacuum would prevent the transfer of heat from the outside. To further insulate the flasks, he silvered them. The silver coating prevented the absorption of radiant energy from the outside and the escape of cold from the inside.

Using his invention, Dewar successfully liquefied **oxygen** in 1885 and became the first person to liquefy **hydrogen** in 1898. His original vacuum bottle was made of glass, but later models were made of metal, which was stronger and made larger models possible.

Dewar did not patent his vacuum flask. It was not until 1904 that Reinhold Burger realized its potential for use in the home, since it kept cold liquids cold and hot liquids hot. Burger offered a prize for a name. *Thermos,* the Greek word for "hot," won.

Modern vacuum bottles (or thermoses) are constructed with walls of glass or steel. The stopper and internal support are made of cork, which

The vacuum bottle has had uses far beyond those imagined by its creator, Scottish chemist James Dewar.

helps to insulate as well. If the bottle is dropped, however, one or both of the walls of the container can shatter. This destroys the vacuum, allowing air to enter and destroying the bottle's ability to insulate. Vacuum bottles do not "make" their contents hot or cold, they merely maintain the temperature of the contents when put into the flask.

. Valence

In 1799 French chemist Joseph Louis Proust was the first to recognize that chemical compounds (mixtures) may have a definite and constant make-up. Proust formally stated this in his law of constant composition. This law raised the possibility that elements may have certain characteristic tendencies to combine with each other. One gram of **hydrogen**, for example, was known always to combine with eight grams of **oxygen** in the formation of water.

After British chemist John Dalton published his statement of the **atomic theory** in 1808, Proust's law could be expressed in terms of atoms. That is, each type of atom appeared to have some specific tendency to combine with other atoms.

The first clear statement of this idea appeared in about 1852. It was made possible by advances in the techniques of chemical analysis and clarification of the relationship among atoms, molecules, and chemical formulas.

The research that finally led to a modern theory of valence (or valency) was British chemist Edward Frankland's study of organometallic compounds. Organometallic compounds consist of a metal combined with one or more organic groups. Frankland found that each metal he studied would combine with only a fixed number of organic groups. For zinc, for example, that number was two. He concluded that "the combining power of the attracting element, if I may be allowed the term, is always satisfied by the same number of these atoms." By *combining power,* Frankland was referring to the concept that was later called "quantivalence," or "valency," or "valence."

It is somewhat surprising that the concept of valence grew out of organic chemistry. Organic compounds are, in general, much more complex than are inorganic compounds.

The next step in valence theory was Alexander W. Williamson's (1824-1904) idea that certain specific atoms were needed to hold other atoms together in a molecule. He showed, for example, that one oxygen atom could hold two hydrogen atoms together in a water molecule.

German chemist Friedrich Kekulé used Williamson's research in his 1858 analysis of organic compounds. Kekulé came to the conclusion that the carbon atom is always tetravalent (that is, always combines with four other atoms, no more and no less). He developed symbols to represent this combining power, or valency, of the carbon atom.

At least one important problem remained with valence theory: the possibility of variable valences. Sulfur, for example, appears to have a valence of two in hydrogen sulfide, four in sulfur dioxide, and six in sulfuric acid. How could one atom exhibit so many different degrees of "saturation capacity," or valence?

A number of ingenious solutions were proposed for this dilemma. But it was not until the concepts of ionic and covalent (the sharing of a pair of electrons by two atoms) chemical bonding were developed in the twentieth century that this problem was satisfactorily resolved.

James Van Allen designed the small instrument package on Explorer 1 *that first identified the large bands of radiation circling Earth.*

⋆⋆ Van Allen belts

When *Explorer 1,* the first U.S. satellite, was launched in early 1958, it carried miniaturized instruments designed to study the regions surrounding Earth in space. James Van Allen, an expert on cosmic rays and skilled with electronic miniaturization technology, designed the small instrument package that orbited over 600 miles above Earth.

One of the most interesting findings of *Explorer 1* involved radiation levels surrounding Earth. Van Allen believed that the satellite had found a large band of radiation too intense for the detector to register. If true, this was discouraging news because it meant that humans would not survive a space flight without heavy shielding.

In the hopes of finding out just how intense the radiation was, Van Allen designed a special Geiger counter (an instrument used to measure radioactivity) for *Explorer 4*. As the satellite orbited Earth many times, it drew the shape of the radiation belt using information it relayed to the ground. These high levels of radiation formed a band around Earth at the equator, but curved toward Earth's surface near the polar regions. The overall shape of this band was not unlike a fat doughnut with the hole along Earth's axis, and followed the theorized shape of **Earth's magnetic field**.

Measurements taken by the moon-bound *Pioneer 3* later revealed two distinct belts. These belts of radiation came to be known as the Van Allen belts since it was Van Allen's interest in cosmic rays that led to the findings.

Origin of the Belts

Scientists felt that the belts were probably composed of charged particles that originated in the **Sun** and became trapped in Earth's magnetic field. This theory was confirmed in 1958 when charged particles from an atmospheric nuclear test temporarily formed an "induced" radiation belt, following the behavior predicted for such particles.

Today little doubt about the origin of the Van Allen belts remains, although the reason for the existence of two belts is not completely understood. The **solar wind**, in interaction with the belts, creates the beautiful auroras (northern and southern lights) near the poles during periods of high solar activity, usually around sunspot maximum. The interaction between the magnetic field and the upper atmosphere also may have an effect on the **ozone** holes found high in the Earth's stratosphere.

Velcro

The bigger the piece of Velcro you have, the more sheer strength there is.

Velcro is a fabric-strip fastener that takes the place of **zippers**, **buttons**, hooks, and snaps. It was invented by Swiss engineer Georges de Mestral. One day in 1948, while returning from hunting in the Alps (a mountain range in southern Europe), de Mestral noticed burrs sticking to his clothing and his dog. He placed a burr under a microscope and discovered that it consisted of hundreds of tiny hooks that would catch and hold onto anything that had loops.

De Mestral designed a fastener that worked on the burr principle. It took him ten years to perfect his invention, which consisted simply of two strips of woven **nylon**, one containing thousands of tiny hooks and the other thousands of tiny loops. When pressed together, the strips cling to one another, just like burrs to clothing. The strips could be stuck together and separated thousands of times.

De Mestral called his invention Velcro, from the French *velours,* "velvet," and *crochet,* "small hook." Velcro was patented worldwide in 1957. The basic patent ran out in 1978, so competing brands are now manufactured. However, the name remains a registered trademark, so only the original can be called "velcro." The material is used in an amazing variety of applications, from the U.S. space program to shoelace replacement.

Velcro is extremely strong, so the bigger the piece of Velcro you have, the more sheer strength there is. This makes possible Velcro jumping, or leaping off a **trampoline** wearing Velcro-hook coveralls and sticking to a Velcro-loop-covered wall. This feat was demonstrated on **television** by talk show host David Letterman.

⋆ Venus

The first person to see Venus with a telescope was the Italian scientist Galileo Galilei.

Venus is the second planet from the **Sun**. Together with **Mercury**, Venus is an "inferior" planet—one whose orbit is nearer to the Sun than the Earth's orbit is. Venus is often called Earth's "sister planet" because it is the closest planet to Earth and because the two planets are nearly identical in size and mass. Venus gets its name from the Roman goddess of love and beauty because, viewed from Earth, it is one of the most brilliant objects in the sky.

Although Venus was observed at least as far back as Mesopotamian times (3500 B.C.), the first person to see Venus with a telescope was the Italian scientist **Galileo Galilei** (1564-1642). He immediately recognized and recorded its different phases, which are like those of the **Moon**, going from a thin crescent to a full disk.

Scientists set to work to learn more about Venus. By 1640 the planet's orbital period was established as 224.7 Earth days (Earth's orbital period is 365 days). A major problem that occupied astronomers for centuries was measuring the period of Venus's daily rotation. In 1667 Italian-born French astronomer Gian Dominico Cassini followed an especially bright spot coming from Venus and concluded that its daily rotation was 23 hours (Earth's is 24 hours).

In 1761 astronomers observed during a transit (when a planet passes in front of the Sun) that Venus had a dense atmosphere of thick, luminous clouds. Many scientists believed that these thick clouds were composed of water vapor and that Venus, therefore, must be a swamp-like planet overrun with vegetation. This image survived until the twentieth century, when a radically different view of Venus emerged.

In the 1920s, astronomers Charles Edward St. John and Seth Barnes Nicholson used a spectroscope to determine that the clouds surrounding Venus did not contain water. They also observed that Venus had a dry, desert-like surface. This claim was supported by Rupert Wildt who in 1937 discovered that Venus's atmosphere contained high amounts of **carbon dioxide** but very little **oxygen** or water vapor.

In the 1950s, **radio** waves emitted by Venus indicated that it had an extremely hot surface temperature. Scientists today recognize Venus as a supreme example of the greenhouse effect. Energy from the Sun becomes trapped by the dense carbon dioxide gases in the atmosphere, heating the surface temperature of Venus to well over ten times that of Earth.

What the Space Probes Showed

In the early 1960s, both the Soviet Union and the United States began extensive space exploration of Venus. In 1961 the Soviet Union launched *Venera 1,* the first spacecraft to be sent to another planet. Unfortunately, radio contact was lost after two weeks and the *Venera 1* mission failed. The U.S. spacecraft, *Mariner 2,* launched in 1962, was the first successful flight to Venus. Although it only came within 22,000 miles of the planet, *Mariner 2* sent back important information. It found cold, dense clouds in the upper atmosphere, a surface temperature of 800° F (426° C), and a water vapor level of only 1/1,000 of Earth's. It also determined that Venus had no **magnetic field**. The Soviet Union succeeded in sending probes to the planet's surface in the 1970s. They measured a surface temperature of 900° F (482° C) and a pressure of 90 atmospheres, which is equal to a crushing pressure of $^2/_3$ ton per square inch.

The first photographs of Venus were taken in 1975 when *Venera 9* and *Venera 10* landed on Venus. *Venera 9* transmitted images back to Earth for approximately 50 minutes, revealing sharp, angular rocks all around the landing site. *Venera 10,* launched less than a week later, transmitted for 60 minutes, sending back photographs that show older, more weathered rock formations.

In 1978 the United States launched *Pioneer Venus 1* and *Pioneer Venus 2. Venus 1* mapped 90 percent of Venus's surface, revealing great mountain ranges, vast plateaus, and expansive plains. *Venus 2* measured atmospheric conditions.

In the early 1980s, the United States laid the groundwork for the *Magellan* program. *Magellan* was launched aboard a **space shuttle** on May 4, 1989, and began orbiting Venus fourteen months later. Using a sophisticated **radar** system, *Magellan* sent back images of Venus that have three times the resolution power of earlier orbiters. Whereas previous photographs showed surface features over 180 miles, *Magellan* can return images as small as one mile across.

These detailed pictures have greatly advanced scientific knowledge of Venus's geological history. Scientists have discovered that, as on Earth, volcanic activity and tectonic faulting (plate movement) have created Venus's complex and varied landscape. Barring technical problems, the *Magellan* orbiter is expected to continue sending back valuable information about Earth's sister planet well into the 1990s.

See also **Plate tectonics**

✦ Video game

The field of electronics has greatly improved modern life. Consider the telephone system, street lights, or automatic bank machines, for example. Electronics has also advanced more fun things in life—such as games.

The concept of video games began in 1966. Ralph Baer, an engineer at a military firm, thought of the 60 million **television** sets in the United States at that time. All they were being used for was to show programs such as news and sports. Baer thought, what if he could figure out something else to do with televisions besides showing programs?

So he invented a very simple game with one spot chasing another one around the screen. Next he and his friends invented a paddle and ball game, and after that a video hockey game. After they received a patent for their creations in 1972, they licensed their inventions to the television giant, Magnavox, and the video game industry was born.

Video games really took off with video cartridges designed for use in the home with TV sets.

The game Pong was invented in 1972 by Noland Buschnel. This was an electronic tennis game. Buschnel founded his own company known as Atari. Another popular early game was PacMan.

At first, video games were usually played in arcades, where machines that took coins were set up. Video games really took off with video cartridges designed for use in the home with TV sets.

Two of the most popular of these video cartridge machines are Super Nintendo and Sega Genesis. These machines sell for around $100 to $200 and are designed to be hooked up to a TV screen. There are also hand-held machines such as Game Boy or Game Gear that take smaller cartridges and display on a very small screen. Personal computer-based games and compact disc (CD-ROM) games are a fairly recent innovation.

The best video games are created by talented computer programmers and software designers. A rich variety of games have been produced. Examples of these are Super Mario, Tetris, Donkey Kong, Sonic the Hedgehog, and Mortal Kombat. Electronic Arts is a major American company producing video games.

Many billion dollars' worth of video games are now being sold every year. Some experts say that more money is spent on buying video games than on going to movies in theaters. Because of this popularity, a lot of people are interested in getting involved in making or planning video games.

Cable television channels and "online" computer networks also have plans to distribute video games over TV sets or personal computers. From your TV set or personal computer, you will be able to look at hundreds of games without having to buy individual cartridges. In some cases, people from all over the country or the world can play against each other over the network, as if they were in the same room.

See also **Computer input and output devices; Computer speech recognition; Microcomputer; Optical disk; Voice synthesizer**

⋆⋆⋆ Video recording

The very first device to record a video signal was developed by British inventor John Logie Baird in 1928. Laird's invention used a 78 r.p.m. (revolutions per minute) disc identical to those used in audio recording to store video information. However, his device was not very practical, and his design became obsolete (out of date). Scientists went to work on an affordable machine for the recording and playback of video signals.

First Machines Debut

The first such machines were introduced in 1948. Their main drawback was that they unwound at a very high speed, so they required a huge supply of thick, heavy magnetic tape. Another problem was that the machines could not maintain a constant speed, resulting in interference and signal loss.

In 1951 Alexander M. Poniatoff assembled a team of scientists at his California laboratory to design what would eventually become the prototype (first version) video tape recorder. By 1954 the team had developed a recorder with a stationary (non-moving) head that eliminated the need for large quantities of tape. They demonstrated their machine to the Ampex company in 1955. On November 30, 1956, it was used in the first retransmission of a recorded **television** program. Retransmission allowed a California television station to rebroadcast that day's showing of *Douglas Edwards and the News*.

For more than a decade, Ampex was the premier designer of video recording technology. They introduced the first color video recorder in 1958.

Another American company, 3M, was responsible for the first mass production of video magnetic tape. Two 3M employees, Mel Sater and Joe Mazzitello, knew of Ampex's plans to introduce their recording machine into the general market in 1956. Working long, hours, they managed to present their own invention on the very same day Ampex's recorder hit the stores.

The next generation of video recording devices will most likely use laser discs in place of magnetic tapes.

Innovations Follow

In 1966 Ampex created the Videofile system, which used a video tape recorder to store up to 200,000 documents on a reel of tape. In 1967 Ampex created a short-term, quick-access recorder. It could record for only 30 seconds at a time, but it allowed an operator to locate and display segments in only four seconds. This machine found a use as an instant-replay recorder. Ampex also designed the cartridge-loading recorders that are used to play very short recordings such as commercials and news briefs.

Japanese Dominate Market

Since the late 1950s, video technology has been dominated by Japanese producers. In 1958 Toshiba produced the first single-head recorder. This was followed the next year by the two-head machine manufactured by Japan Victor Company (JVC) and in 1964 by the Sony Corporation's marketing of the very first video tape recorder for home use.

With more and more people using them, it became necessary for the many video tape recorder producers to agree upon certain standards, especially the style of videotape. In 1970 the Philips Company finished its newest project: a video cassette recorder, or VCR. The enclosed cassette design replaced the old, bulky reel-to-reel systems. Within two years JVC and Matsushita, working jointly, developed a cassette using a ³/₄-inch tape that quickly became the industry standard.

As more and more people purchased VCRs for use at home, they demanded a machine that could be used to film home movies as well as television broadcasts. The first home video cameras came in two varieties, those with separate recorders and those with built-in recording machines. The second type, though, was not well received by the public. It used small "micro cassettes" that could not be played on a home VCR. Newer models use a standard cassette for both recording and playback.

What's in Store

The next generation of video recording devices will most likely use laser discs in place of magnetic tapes. Somewhat like John Logie Baird's 1928 "video album," the videodisc player uses a weak laser to read tiny bumps on the disc's surface. A typical videodisc can hold several hours of video information and thousands of pages of text—all of which can be instantly accessed. Models that allow playback but cannot record are currently available for home use.

See also **Magnetic recording; Optical disk**

⋆⋆⋆ Vinyl

Vinyl is a chemical made from **ethylene**. The term "vinyl" refers to a group of different compounds (mixtures) with a similar structure. Examples of vinyls include: polyvinyl chloride, polyvinyl acetate, polyvinylidene chloride, polyvinyl alcohol, polyvinylacetals, polyvinyl fluoride, polyvinyl pyrrolidone, polyvinylcarbazole, and polyvinyl ethers.

PVC

Probably the most familiar of these vinyls is polyvinyl chloride (PVC). PVC is weather-resistant, is an excellent electrical insulator, and is nonflammable. Today both rigid and plasticized PVC are in great demand. Both are often used in copolymers (a **polymer** of two different monomers), most commonly copolymers of vinyl chloride and vinyl acetate. These have been used in everything from records to vinyl floor tiles. Rigid PVC is ideal for pipes. Plasticized PVC is used in garden hoses, imitation leather, raincoats, and electric plugs.

See also **Polymer and polymerization; Waterproof material**

★ Virus

Viruses are tiny particles that consist mainly of protein and nucleic acid. They are able to reproduce, but since they lack **cell** structure and the ability to metabolize food, viruses can reproduce only inside other living host

The AIDS virus attacking a T-4 lymphocyte. Viruses are very adaptable and are found throughout the biosphere.

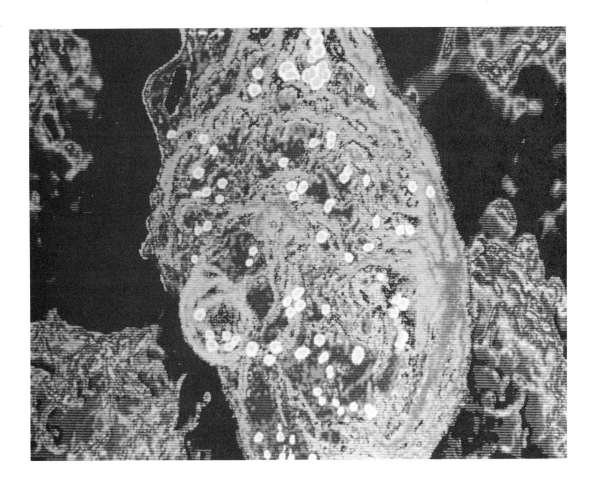

Viruses are very adaptable and are found throughout the biosphere, from the viruses that causes AIDS, chicken pox, and measles in humans, to the viruses that live within plants and cause tobacco leaves to wilt and tulips to turn bright colors.

cells. Viruses, which are far smaller than the smallest **bacteria**, can be crystallized, much as a mineral forms a crystalline structure. Thus viruses are not considered alive but do show one characteristic of living things when in a host cell—they reproduce. Viruses are very adaptable and are found throughout the biosphere, from the viruses that causes **AIDS**, chicken pox, and measles in humans, to the viruses that live within plants and cause tobacco leaves to wilt and tulips to turn bright colors.

Bacteria Search Leads to Viruses

The existence of viruses was only hypothesized a little over 100 years ago. In the late nineteenth century, Louis Pasteur, the notable French chemist and microbiologist, hypothesized that there might be pathogenic (harmful) organisms smaller than bacteria. After much experience culturing (growing) bacteria, he turned his attention to rabies, a serious infectious disease caused by viruses and transmitted through the bites of infected animals. In 1885 Pasteur weakened the rabies germ by passing a rabies infection through different species of animals until it was less virulent (deadly). His preparation was complete when a nine-year-old boy was brought to him for treatment. The boy had been bitten and mauled by a mad dog and Pasteur's preparation of weakened germs saved the boy's life. This triumph over rabies was one of the crowning achievements of Pasteur's career, yet the great scientist was perplexed at not being able to locate the germ that causes rabies. It was a virus—too small to see with his compound light microscope.

Simultaneously, one of Pasteur's associates, Charles-Edouard Chamberland, was working on a number of technical advances that made bacterial research more efficient. He introduced the autoclave, an airtight heating device that could be used for killing bacteria. He also improved laboratory filters, making them out of unglazed porcelain. They were well-suited for filtering out bacteria.

Chamberland's filters were used by Dmitri Ivanovsky, a Russian botanist (plant scientist) who in 1892 was the first to demonstrate that some pathogenic agents smaller than bacteria were linked to disease. He crushed tobacco leaves that were infected with the tobacco mosaic disease, a disease that stunts tobacco plants and creates a mottled, mosaic pattern on their leaves. He filtered the sap released by the infected leaves and when he added the sap to healthy plants, they, too, got the disease. Ivanovsky concluded that either tiny particles in the sap were responsible for transmitting the disease or there was something wrong with his filtration system. However, he mistakenly thought that anything that went through the filters must be minuscule bacteria.

Just six years later, Dutch bacteriologist Martinus Willem Beijerinck was continuing the search for the cause of tobacco mosaic disease. He confirmed Ivanovsky's findings but concluded that the infection of tobacco was not caused by bacteria but by a much smaller organism, a "virus"—a term that Beijerinck coined. *Virus* is a Latin word for "poison." In that same year, another scientist, Friedrich August Löffler, showed that a virus caused foot-and-mouth disease in livestock.

The Nature of Viruses

It was not until the 1930s that the crystalline nature of viruses was discovered. Experiments suggested that the virus itself was not a living thing, just as an enzyme is in itself not alive. However, the virus does reproduce when within living cells. The discovery of something that straddled the border between living and nonliving stirred up arguments that continue even today about what is alive and what is not.

Work with viruses in the past had often been contaminated by bacteria, but in the 1940s, **antibiotics** made it possible to grow viruses free from bacterial contamination. This method made possible the study of the mumps virus and the virus that causes chicken pox. A variation of this method was used to develop a vaccine against the poliomyelitis (polio) virus.

Research since the 1960s has uncovered numerous groups of viruses. The very largest, such as the virus that causes smallpox, are more complex in structure and contain double-stranded **DNA (deoxyribonucleic acid)**. The smallest viruses, the picornaviruses, include the viruses that cause the common cold and polio. They are hundreds of times smaller than poxviruses and have a very geometric polyhedral shape. Other groups of viruses in between vary in size, shape, and the presence or absence or a tail or a protective envelope.

Research in the 1970s and 1980s has uncovered two other groups of particles even smaller than viruses that replicate only when inside a living cells. Viroids enter a plant cell host and lodge in the cell nucleus, where they interfere in some way with cell function. Viroids are responsible for plant diseases that have ravaged certain crops as diverse as coconut trees in the Philippines and chrysanthemums in the United States. Another group of particles similar in behavior to viruses are prions, which enter cells and can cause certain rare nervous disorders in humans and animals.

In the 1940s, antibiotics made it possible to grow viruses free from bacterial contamination. This method made possible the study of the mumps virus and the virus that causes chicken pox. A variation of this method was used to develop a vaccine against polio

⋆⋆ Vitamin

Vitamins are organic compounds (mixtures made from living organisms such as plant and animal **tissue**). The human body needs vitamins to work properly and for good health. We acquire almost all of the 13 compounds classified as vitamins from the foods we eat. A small number, however—

James Lind giving oranges and lemons to a sailor suffering from scurvy. The continued lack of any vitamin, even in an otherwise adequate diet, usually leads to a deficiency disease such as scurvy.

How Vitamins Got Their Names and Letters

In the early part of the twentieth century, Polish biochemist Casimir Funk studied the various "accessory food factors" that had already been identified. He suggested they be named "vitamines" or "amine compounds vital for life." (Amines are organic compounds of **nitrogen**.) After it became clear that not all these compounds were amines, the final "e" was dropped from vitamines.

At about the same time, American biochemists Elmer V. McCollum and Thomas B. Osborne, working independently, isolated a growth-producing substance in egg yolks that appeared quite different from the water-soluble vitamins already discovered. In 1916 McCollum went on to show that at least two factors were responsible for the normal growth of rats, factors he named "fat-soluble A" and "water-soluble B." McCollum is therefore credited with initiating the custom of labeling vitamins by letters.

including biotin and vitamin K—are at least partially synthesized (created) by the body itself.

Vitamins are generally divided into two groups: fat-soluble and water-soluble. Fat-soluble vitamins include vitamins A, D, E and K. Vitamin B, which is actually a group of eight similar compounds, and vitamin C are water-soluble.

Although vitamins are not all chemically related, they share the same basic purpose: to help regulate the processes the body uses to convert food into energy and living tissues (metabolism). Most of the vitamins accomplish this by acting as **enzymes**. They alter molecules and cause chemical reactions while remaining unchanged themselves. Several of the vitamins, however—including all those in the B family—are inactive until converted into coenzymes. Coenzymes are organic substances that usually contain a vitamin or mineral and combine with a protein to form an active enzyme system. For example, the B, B_2 and B_6 molecules become activated by the addition of phosphate groups.

Only tiny amounts of each vitamin are needed to ensure **metabolism**, but these tiny amounts are absolutely essential. The continued lack of any vitamin, even in an otherwise adequate diet, usually leads to a deficiency disease, such as pellagra (from a lack of nicotinic acid—a B vitamin),

Are Supplemental Vitamins Necessary?

Many people think they can improve their health by taking vitamin pills. Most medical experts believe this is unnecessary. They say that eating a varied diet of fresh food and exposing the skin to enough sunlight to increase vitamin D reserves (but not enough to burn the skin) should provide enough vitamins under most circumstances. In fact, too much of some vitamins can cause problems.

beriberi (from a lack of vitamin B_1 [thiamin]), or scurvy (from a lack of vitamin C [ascorbic acid]). Vitamins were discovered, in fact, because scientists had been looking for centuries for the causes of these deficiency diseases. Until relatively recently, they searched in the wrong direction.

See also **Digestion**

⋆⋆⋆ Voice synthesizer

Many of us are familiar with synthesizers, machines with simple keyboards that duplicate the sounds of musical instruments. The earliest known machine that duplicated the sound of a human voice was developed in 1778 by Wolfgang von Kempelen. Eyewitnesses reported that it could speak several words in a timid, childlike voice. Although the machine appeared real, Baron von Kempelen was known for being a slippery character. Nine years earlier, he had built a chess-playing machine, which defeated many players, including the French Emperor Napoleon. Eventually it was discovered that the machine was a fraud—its cabinet concealed a hidden, human chess player.

In 1830 Austrian professor Joseph Faber produced his own speaking automaton. (Automaton is from the Latin for self-operating machine. It refers to something that acts in a mechanical way.) Faber's machine, Euphonia, took 25 years to construct. Euphonia could recite the alphabet, whisper, laugh, and ask "How do you do?"—all in English with a German accent. Speech was produced by a complicated set of inner workings.

The first talking machines using electronic technology were developed in the 1930s. The Voice Operation Demonstrator, or Voder, could imitate human speech and even speak complete sentences as its operator pressed keys on a board. The technology evolved further with the rapid development of computers in the 1950s. During the late 1960s, the MITalk System was developed at the Massachusetts Institute of Technology in Cambridge, Massachusetts. Although originally designed as a reading machine for the blind, once completed, the system could convert nearly any type of text into speech-synthesized output.

Raymond Kurzweil produced the Kurzweil reading machine in 1976. It could read everything from a phone bill to a full-length novel and provided unlimited-vocabulary synthesized output. Sometimes called a set of eyes for the blind, the reading machine has proved very popular.

Today, speech synthesis is a useful way to convey information in public places. Cars, appliances, and even games are being equipped with voice-synthesizer chips. A recently developed "talking chessboard" plays an amateurish game of chess and announces each move it makes.

See also **Computer input and output devices; Video game**

Raymond Kurzweil produced the Kurzweil reading machine in 1976. The machine converts printed words into synthetic speech.

Walkman

In the 1970s, small **audiocassettes** replaced eight-track tapes as the tape format preferred by consumers. At the time, small cassette recorders with built-in speakers were already on the market, but the audio quality was poor.

In 1979 Akio Morita, president of Sony Corporation, created a pocket-sized cassette player using the miniaturized electronic parts pioneered, in part, by his own company. This pocket-sized player, called the "Walkman," featured tiny motors and a miniature circuit board housed in a plastic casing. It came equipped with lightweight headphones that allowed listeners to take the instrument almost anywhere. The Walkman proved so popular that other varieties appeared, including models with AM-FM **radios**, recording capability, and, recently, models that play compact discs.

Washing machine

Before the invention of the washing machine, clothes were cleaned by soaking them in stream water and pounding them with rocks. In 1797 the invention of the washboard for scrubbing eliminated the need for the rocks.

Hundreds of mechanical washing machines were designed in the first half of the nineteenth century, but they were hand powered. The earliest models rubbed clothes to clean them. Later designs featured mechanisms that moved the clothes through the water. The user either turned a handle to rotate or rock the washing box or pumped a wooden dolly to stir the clothes.

Steam power was applied to commercial washing machines in the 1850s. An enterprising California gold miner used his machine to wash shirts in exchange for gold dust. Brother David Parker of the Canterbury, New Hampshire, Shaker religious community patented his "Wash-Mill" for hotel use in 1858. By 1880, 4,000 to 5,000 different washing machine designs had been patented. But most home washing machines remained hand powered until the early 1900s.

Electric and Automatic Washers

Electric washing machines first appeared in the early 1900s. Electric wringer washers appeared in 1910. Wringer washers required that soaking-wet clothes be removed and forced through a pair of rollers to extract the water. In 1911 the Maytag Company introduced its electric Hired Girl wringer washer. These early electric washers were adaptable to gasoline power and could be hand operated as well. A wringerless model was marketed as early as 1926 by the Easy Washing Machine Company, but wringer washers continued to be the industry standard until the 1950s.

The automatic washing machine was introduced in 1937 by Bendix. Their Model S required only two settings of the dial during its cycles, although the machine vibrated so ferociously it had to be bolted to the floor. A fully automatic Bendix appeared in 1947. The market was flooded with other machines following World War II (1939-45) to satisfy postwar demand for consumer products.

Spin-dry machines overtook the old wringer types in popularity by 1953. Most machines that were manufactured in the mid-1950s featured lint filters, bleach and soap dispensers, and speed selection. By 1958, 90 percent of all American households used electric washing machines.

The contemporary washing machine offers many options so the user can adjust the wash to the garment being washed. For example, the user can select cycles for permanent press, synthetic, or delicate fabrics. A range of temperatures can be selected for both wash and rinse cycles. Length of cycles and prewash and soak options can be chosen. Modern washing machines are either front loading or top loading.

. Waterbed

Waterbeds were mentioned in the 1961 science fiction novel *Stranger in a Strange Land* by Robert A. Heinlein. The concept was not actually applied until 1965. Then two physicians, James Weinstein and Barry Davidson, designed a water-filled mattress for use by hospital patients.

During the 1960s and 1970s, the waterbed gained popularity, beginning with young people known as "hippies" and gradually working its way into mainstream American society. The bed was proclaimed ideal for sleeping, but its detractors claimed it a hazard because of its weight (about 1800 pounds [817 kg]) and the possibility of leakage or—worse yet—electrocution if electricity came in contact with the bed's water. Despite these risks, U.S. sales reached $3.4 million by 1984.

. Waterproof material

Ever since people began wearing clothing and going out in the rain, they have tried to find a way to keep water from soaking through their clothes. Early waterproofing methods relied on the natural properties of the fabrics being worn. For example, wool was treated with lanolin emulsions. Lanolin is a fatty substance obtained from wool. It boosted the water repellency of the naturally occurring oil in the wool. Cotton was treated with a wax emulsion. These treatments were inexpensive, but they washed out when the fabric was cleaned.

In 1823 Scottish chemist Charles Macintosh patented his method of producing rainproof cloth using **rubber**. He coated one side of wool cloth with a liquid rubber solution, then covered it with another piece of wool cloth. Since rain could not penetrate the rubber, the inner layer of garments made with Macintosh's material remained dry. The rainproof coats made by Macintosh's company became known as mackintoshes.

An American inventor named Otis Ferrin patented a waterproof "painting cloth" in the mid-1800s. His process applied heavy oil to heavy material. The resulting waterproof fabric became known as oilcloth and was used worldwide for table coverings and raingear for well over 100 years before being replaced by **plastics**.

Advances in chemistry gave rise to new water-repellent finishes. **Silicones** are one type. They are more expensive than the waxes but can stand

Invention of Scotch-gard and Gore-Tex

Scotch-gard was an accidental invention of the ever-productive Minnesota Mining and Manufacturing Company (3M) research lab. An assistant in the lab accidentally spilled an experimental fluid on her canvas sneaker. She found that she could not remove the substance but the affected sneaker stayed cleaner than its mate.

Lab chemists Patsy Sherman and Samuel Smith sensed possibilities. They launched the experiments that produced Scotch-gard, first marketed in 1956. When applied to upholstery, rainwear, and clothing—either by the manufacturer or by the consumer—Scotch-gard makes a fabric stain-resistant by making the material shed rather than absorb liquids. Today, Scotch-gard is the world's most-sold protective finish for leather, fabrics, and **carpeting**, and is now being used on wood as well.

Gore-Tex was invented by W. L. Gore and Bob Gore. W. L. Gore left the Du Pont company in 1958 to devote himself full-time to developing the company's Teflon product into insulation for computer wiring. Meanwhile, his son Bob earned a Ph.D. in chemical engineering and joined his father's lab. One day in 1969, Bob yanked a rod of Teflon instead of gently and slowly pulling it. The rod stretched into a porous, strong filament. This expanded Teflon was named Gore-Tex. It was ideal for transmitting computer signals and for use in surgical implants. A Teflon film was bonded to a synthetic fabric to produce a waterproof material that is now widely used in outdoor activity garments and raingear.

up to cleaning. Another type is Scotch-gard. The 1980s saw the birth of a new type of waterproof fabric, which uses its own microscopic structure rather than a chemical finish to repel water. The best-known of these is Gore-Tex.

⋆⋆ Wave motion, law of

Everyday, everywhere we go, we are surrounded by waves. The sounds we hear are carried through the air in waves. The heat we receive from the **Sun** arrives in waves. Even the light reflected from this book travels toward your eyes in waves. It took scientists thousands of years to realize the importance of wave motion, and even longer to truly understand the behavior of waves. Today, a single mathematical equation is all that is needed to understand wave motion.

The first attempt to mathematically describe wave motion was made by Jean Le Rond d'Alembert in 1747. His equation sought to explain the motion of vibrating strings. While d'Alembert's equation was correct, it was overly simplistic.

In 1749 the wave equation was improved upon by Leonhard Euler. He began to apply d'Alembert's theories to all wave forms, not just strings. For more than 70 years the equations of Euler and d'Alembert were debated among the European scientific community, most of whom disagreed upon the universality of their mathematics. Universality means that a particular law applies in all situations.

In 1822 Jean-Baptiste-Joseph Fourier proved that an equation governing all waves could be written. The final equation was provided by John William Strutt (Lord Rayleigh) in 1877, and it is his law of wave motion that is used today.

All wave forms have three physical characteristics in common—wavelength, frequency, and velocity.

Common Features of Waves

All waves have certain properties in common. They all carry some form of energy, whether it is mechanical, electromagnetic, or some other type. They all require some point of origin—an energy source. Almost all move through some sort of medium such as air or water. The exception is **electromagnetic waves**, which travel most efficiently through a vacuum.

All wave forms have three physical characteristics in common—wavelength, frequency, and velocity. This common bond is the reason that the wave equation applies to all wave types.

See also **Electromagnetism; Light, theories of; Ultrasonic wave**

⋆⋆ Weather forecasting model

Weather forecasting has become a much more precise science with the use of mathematical models. Using computers, weather forecasters or meteorologists develop mathematical models that are the crucial link between data collection and weather prediction. Without models and the computers needed to work them, the accuracy and volume of modern data collection could not be used to make accurate predictions.

Forecasting models evolved from the discovery of patterns in atmospheric movement. In particular, new discoveries of air mass and frontal structures (for example, cold fronts) showed that there were causes and effects in weather that could be translated into more accurate forecasts. These discoveries were made in the early part of the twentieth century, and resulted in advances in communications and upper atmospheric research.

Modeling Helps Advance Meteorology

To make better predictions, scientists studied locations over given lengths of time, collecting data about the weather they observed. By studying these long-term trends, meteorologists began to develop an accurate

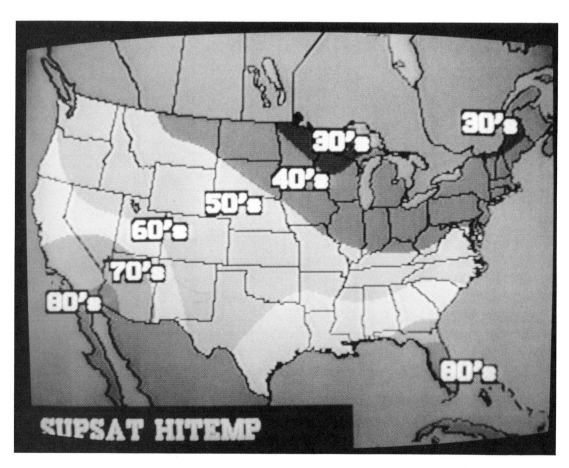

idea of what might happen next over a period of a few days, and how probable that occurrence was.

Even after mathematical modeling became possible, it did not become a practical method until the development of computers in the 1940s. Before that, it took perhaps months or years to manually calculate a reliable 24-hour weather forecast.

Today computers are interconnected with recording stations and remote sensing units (**radar** and satellites), and are capable of making millions of calculations per second. Despite this dramatic increase in capability, two problems continue. One is the timeliness of forecasts. The value of a forecast deteriorates rapidly with time. Warnings of wind sheer to pilots or of tornadoes to the general public are not always received in time to avoid disasters.

The other problem is that models have not been able to deal with the nagging problem of long-range forecasts. Over longer periods, the apparently infinite number of possible interactions within the atmosphere and between the atmosphere and other influences makes it impossible to make long-range forecasts with the same degree of accuracy as short-range forecasts.

Tools Used in Forecasting

With the development of telegraph networks during the 1800s, meteorologists were able to make ground-level observations and forecasts. But they knew little about what was occurring in the upper atmosphere, and so forecasters could not take into account vertical gradients of temperature and barometric pressure, two key elements in the development of **storms** and other weather events.

Widespread use of high-altitude **kites** produced only minor benefits. Only with the regular use of unmanned balloons, with their information-gathering radiosondes (miniature radio transmitters), was accurate forecasting made possible.

Long-range weather forecasting remains an elusive target. Extension of short-range forecasting methods over more than ten days has made the issuance of general outlooks possible at best.

Attention has been given to finding patterns among climatic variations. Researchers search for clues in everything from ancient maps and writings to tree ring growth (dendrochronology). One must keep in mind that what is long-range to a meteorologist is short-range to a climatologist (a scientist who studies weather patterns over hundreds of years).

Weather is the day by day pattern of rain and temperature in a given area. Climate refers to long-term patterns that help us designate certain areas as deserts or tropics.

Weather Forecasting Methods

Modern weather forecasting owes its existence to the invention of many recording weather instruments, such as the barometer, hygrometer, weather balloon, and **radar**. Three major technological developments in particular have led weather forecasting to its current status: the development of instant communications with distant areas beginning in the late 1800s, remote sensing devices starting in the early 1900s, and computers in the late 1900s.

Weather recording instruments date from the fifteenth century when Italian inventor and scientist Leonardo da Vinci invented the hygrometer (hi-grom-e-ter), an instrument that measures atmospheric humidity. About 1643 Italian physicist Evangelista Torricelli created the barometer to measure air pressure differences. These instruments were improved upon in the eighteenth century by Frenchman Jean Andre Deluc and have been refined many times since then.

Weather information has long been displayed in map form. In 1686 English astronomer Edmond Halley drafted a map to explain regular winds, tradewinds, and monsoons. Nearly 200 years later, in 1863, French astronomer Edme Hippolyte Marie-Davy published the first isobar maps, which showed barometric pressure differences.

Weather data allowed scientists to try to forecast what the weather would be at some later time. The U.S. Weather Service was established in 1870 under the supervision of meteorologist Cleveland Abbe, often called America's first weatherman. Telegraph networks made it possible to collect and share weather reports and predictions. By the turn of the twentieth century, the telephone and **radio** further increased meteorologists' ability to collect and exchange information.

Remote sensing, the ability to collect information from unmanned sources, originated with the invention of the weather balloon by Frenchman Leon Teisserenc de Bort (1855-1913). Designed to make

➜

Research currently being conducted on the southern El Niño and La Niña winds could lead to mathematical models of long-range phenomena. It may prove that tracking long-range global cycles in the weather is the answer for making long-range forecasts.

See also **Meteorology; Weather satellite**

simple preflight tests of wind patterns, these balloons were eventually used as complete floating weather stations with the addition of a radio transmitter to the balloon's instruments.

Many scientists added to the pool of meteorological knowledge. In his 1887 book, *Weather,* Englishman Ralph Abercromby depicted a model of a depression (a region of low barometric pressure) that was used for many years. During World War I (1914-18), the father-son team of Vilhelm Bjerknes and Jacob Bjerknes organized a nationwide weather-observing system in their native Norway. With the data available, they formulated the theory of polar fronts: The atmosphere is made up of cold air masses near the poles and warm air masses near the tropics, and fronts exist where these air masses meet.

In the 1940s, Englishman R. C. Sutcliffe and Swede S. Peterssen developed three-dimensional analysis and forecasting methods. American military pilots flying above the Pacific Ocean during World War II (1939-45) discovered a strong stream of air rapidly flowing from west to east, which became known as the jet stream. The development of radar, **rockets**, and satellites greatly improved data collection.

Weather radar first came into use in the United States in 1949 with the efforts of Horace Byers and R. R. Braham. Conventional weather radar shows the location and intensity of precipitation (water or ice droplets). In the 1990s the more advanced Doppler radar, which can continuously measure wind speed and precipitation, came into wide use.

Calculators and computers make it possible for meteorologists to process large amounts of data and make complex calculations quickly. **Weather satellites,** the first launched in 1960, can now produce photographs showing cloud and frontal movements, water-vapor concentrations, and temperature changes. With radar and computer enhancements like coloration, professionals and amateurs alike can better visualize weather information and use it in their daily lives.

Weather satellite

The first attempt to look at earth's weather from space occurred early in the U.S. space program. In 1959 *Vanguard 2* was launched, carrying with

*Satellite photo of
hurricane Gilbert as
it churns its way
through the Gulf of
Mexico toward the
Texas coastline.
Geostationary
Operational
Environmental
Satellites (GOES)
trace hurricanes,
typhoons, and
tropical storms in
the process saving
many lives.*

it light-sensitive cells able to provide information about Earth's cloud cover. Unfortunately, the satellite tumbled in orbit and was unable to return any information. *Explorer VI,* also launched in 1959, was more successful and transmitted the first photographs of Earth's atmosphere from space.

In 1960 the United States launched the first experimental weather satellite, *TIROS 1 (Television and Infra Red Observation Satellite).* *TIROS 1* televised more than 22,000 photos before it failed six weeks later. It detected potential hurricanes days before they could have been spotted by any other means. It watched the spring breakup of the ice in the St. Lawrence River in Canada. It helped forecast weather for the supplying of Antarctic research stations. *TIROS 1* also used infrared detectors to measure the amount of heat radiated by Earth's surface and by the clouds.

Later versions of *TIROS* improved upon the original. Some had television cameras that provided direct, real-time readouts of pictures to weather stations around the world. Others allowed for direct-readout, automatic picture transmission and storage of global images for later trans-

HURRICANE GILBERT
SEPT. 13 1988
6 PM EDT

TEXAS

MEXICO

YUCATAN

mission and processing. Some of these satellites were placed in geo-stationary orbit (moving at the same speed as Earth) and thus were able to continuously observe one area. This helped in the detection of severe storms and tornadoes and provided real-time coverage at an earlier stage of cloud and frontal weather movements.

Other *TIROS*-type satellites are in polar orbit, where their infrared sensors measure temperatures and water vapor over the entire globe. *GOES* (*Geostationary Operational Environmental Satellites*) also cover the western and eastern hemispheres. These satellites can provide weather reports for places that were not covered very well in the past: ocean regions, deserts, and polar areas. They also trace hurricanes, typhoons, and tropical storms, in the process saving many lives. Their data are used to produce state-of-the-art charts showing sea-surface temperatures—information useful to the shipping and fishing industries.

New satellites that probe Earth's atmosphere by day and night in all weather are being developed in many countries. Since the weather satellite is now an established tool of meteorologists all over the world, both developed and developing nations will continue to rely on these crafts.

⋆ Wheelchair

No one knows where or when the first wheelchair was invented. We do know that some one-of-a-kind wheeled chairs were built during the 1600s. Wooden wheelchairs were in use in the United States by the 1860s. The first modern wheelchair—a lightweight folding model—was designed and marketed in 1932 simultaneously by Sam Duke and by the team of Harry C. Jennings, a mechanical engineer, and Herbert Everest, an injured mining engineer.

The electrically powered wheelchair first appeared around the time of World War I (1914-18). However, manually powered wheelchairs remained the norm until the 1960s. Then, the number of quadriplegics (people paralyzed from the neck down) created sufficient demand for wheelchairs propelled in ways other than by hand. There are now electric wheelchairs that can be activated by hand, head movement, tongue, and breath. In 1982 French astronomy student Martine Kempf developed a computer program that responded to voice commands—the Katalavox—which is now used to power both wheelchairs and microscopes.

Improvements in wheelchair durability and maneuverability have fueled a growing interest in wheelchair sports.

Tom Houston, a pipefitter paralyzed by a fall in 1979, designed the HiRider with the help of fellow pipefitter Ray Metzger. This revolutionary wheelchair, which went on the market in 1989, allows the user to maintain a standing position while moving about. Wheelchairs capable of climbing stairs and curbs also are manufactured now.

In 1987 West Germany issued the Rollsteiger. In 1992 the United States issued a high-priced computer-and-sonar-equipped ACCESS Mobility System. Both models use the standard four wheels on flat surfaces but convert to tank-like treads to climb over obstacles.

Improvements in wheelchair durability and maneuverability have fueled a growing interest in wheelchair sports as well.

⋆⋆⋆ Windshield and windshield wiper

Windshields

Early windshield wipers had a timing problem. When the car went fast, the wipers sped up. When the car slowed, the wipers slowed.

Early **automobiles** traveled at fairly slow speeds, so little if any wind-breaking protection was needed or provided. As the speed of vehicles became faster, wind-breaking protection became more important. The earliest "windshields" were nothing more than vertical sheets of plate glass in wooden frames. Plate glass is a strong and polished glass that contains few impurities and is used for large windows and mirrors.

The plate glass proved to be not strong enough, sometimes breaking and causing injury to drivers and passengers. In 1905 inventor John C. Wood tried gluing two sheets of glass together with a central layer of celluloid (a material used to make photographic film). The laminated glass he produced was expensive and hard to make. The celluloid tended to turn yellow over time, which was a safety hazard.

Designers continued to work on laminated glass to make it easier to produce and to eliminate the yellowing. Finally, in 1928, laminated safety glass began to be installed for windshields and side and rear windows. One advantage of laminated glass was that it could be curved to suit specific manufacturing needs, but it usually required a frame. This made it less desirable for automobiles.

A type of toughened glass was developed as an alternative to laminated glass. The French glassmakers St. Gobain developed this hardened glass for car windshields in 1929. Their glass was based on research done at the U.S.-based Owens-Corning company. The glass is super-heated and rapidly cooled in single sheets of glass. When it shatters, it breaks into small, blunt pieces. Toughened glass was found to be more pliable than laminated glass, making it ideal for the curved slopes of the windshield. Unlike laminated glass, it could be fitted directly into the bodywork rather than needing a frame. Unfortunately, the finished product was so rigid that it did not yield upon impact. In the case of an accident where the passenger collides with the windshield, this rigidity could cause severe injury. So development of laminated glass continued. The Triplex company created a curved laminated glass for use in streetcars. In 1956 a British car, the Vauxhall Victor, was fitted with the first wraparound, laminated windshield.

Additional windshield features were developed after World War II (1939-45). These included window defoggers, tinting, and the 1948 introduction by Rolls Royce of **tungsten** wires embedded in the rear window for defogging and de-icing. Tinted glass (under the brand name Sundym), for cutting down on heat and glare, was introduced in American cars years later. To address concerns about safe window glass, car makers created differential zoning, which means windshields will crack and break in such a way that larger undamaged particles will be left in front of the driver.

Wipers

The windshield wiper was created to improve the driver's field of vision. In 1903 a man named J. H. Apjohn invented a system where two

*The windshield and
windshield wiper
were developed for
wind-breaking
protection and to
improve the driver's
field of vision.*

brushes moved up and down the glass. Other systems based on the same principle were later developed using rubber strips rather than brushes.

Before 1917 drivers had to use one hand to manipulate the wipers and the other to steer and shift the car. Ormand Wall, a Hawaiian dentist, recognized the danger in this and installed an electric motor in the middle of the windshield. The motor would swing a long rubber blade across the window. In 1929 another American, William Folberth, designed a wiper that was run by suction from the engine. This type of system had a timing problem, though. When the car went fast, the wipers sped up. When the car slowed, the wipers slowed. By the 1930s, electric-motor wipers were refined and became the standard. In 1933 the British car company Vauxhall produced a blade made up of several short blades controlled by a main curved arm.

⋆⋆ Windsurfer

In the 1960s, two California friends debated the merits of surfing compared to sailing. Hoyle Schweitzer, vice president of a computer firm, argued that sailing was a better sport because surfers had to waste so much time waiting for the right waves and because the shore area was too crowded with other surfers. His friend, Jim Drake, an aeronautical engineer, believed just the opposite. Surfers had the edge, he said, because their sport was so simple and much less time consuming than sailing. Both men began thinking of a way to combine the positive elements of both sports into one new package—a sailing **surfboard**.

In 1967 Drake and Schweitzer tried an enlarged surfboard, but they had problems steering it without a rudder as other boats had. They finally attached the mast to the board with a universal joint. This joint allowed the sail and mast to turn freely in all directions and to lie flat in the water. No other sailing craft is constructed like this one. The two men also created a wishbone-shaped boom that provided support for a standing sailor and allowed him or her to keep the sail extended. They called their creation a "free sail system."

The first board was made of fiberglass, like surfboards of the time. Later, **polyethylene** was used because it was lighter, longer lasting, and less expensive. Today's boards are slightly longer than the traditional surfboard with straps on the top to anchor the feet and a skeg (fin) on the bottom to add stability. They also feature a daggerboard, a small rectangular board, that plunges down through a slot into the water below to keep the board moving straight ahead.

Public reaction was positive and demand was high. Experts called it the first really original sailing idea in 100 years. Hoyle Schweitzer quit his job and devoted himself full time to turning out windsurfers.

⋆⋆ Wind tunnel

Amateur nineteenth-century aviators sometimes studied the flight behavior of birds before building their flying machines. The resulting bird-like craft failed miserably because the builders had no knowledge of lift and drag forces that act on surfaces as they cut through the air.

The earliest invention for testing what happens during flight was a whirling arm. English mathematician Benjamin Robbins first used such a device in the eighteenth century. He mounted objects shaped like pyramids and oblong plates on the arm tip and spun them in different directions. He

Wind tunnel used for testing General Motor's Impact electric car. Wind tunnels allow engineers to study the forces acting on aircraft.

Helium has been used to create a Mach 50 blast of wind.

found that no simple theory would account for the complex forces acting on moving objects. British aviator George Cayley also used a whirling arm to measure drag and lift in the early nineteenth century. The major drawback to whirling arms was the air disturbance they created. The **aircraft** models would fly into their own wakes, so it was impossible to properly study them.

An Englishman, Frank Wenham, is credited with designing and operating the first wind tunnel in 1871. It consisted of a tube 12 feet (4 m) long and 18 inches (about 46 cm) square. A fan driven by a **steam engine** propelled air down the tube to the model aircraft. Wenham soon discovered that wings could support much heavier loads than had been previously thought. Finally, flight was seen as a real possibility.

The Wright Brothers

American inventors and aviators Orville and Wilbur Wright used a wind tunnel to improve their airplanes. The first two gliders they built were unpredictable in the air. They realized that all the scientific information they were using for flight data, which they had gathered from previous experimenters, was wrong. They had to conduct their own investigations.

First they built a square tube for channeling air, a driving **fan**, and a two-part balance mounted in the airstream. They attached various types of wings to the balance. As their contraption revolved, they observed the lifting forces. Later they built a larger and more sophisticated tunnel and got the information they needed for their first manned, powered aircraft.

By the time World War I (1914-18) began, leadership in flight research had shifted to Europe. Many wind tunnels were built there, while facilities in the United States were almost nonexistent. By the 1920s, the growth of aviation spurred renewed interest in American research. The National Advisory Committee for Aeronautics (NACA) began to build wind tunnels. In 1931 NACA started up the world's first full-scale wind tunnel for testing airplanes, a tunnel still in use today. By the end of the 1930s, NACA had created tunnels that allowed engineers to study the forces acting on aircraft near Mach 1 (one times the speed of sound). In 1939 NACA built a high-pressure tunnel that used an 800 horsepower electric motor to drive a propeller, creating a wind speed of 300 miles (48 km) per hour.

After World War II (1939-45), the need for supersonic wind tunnels (faster than the speed of sound) became apparent. These were complicated devices, involving narrowed tunnel walls and compressor fans. In 1948 a supersonic tunnel began providing the data that led to the development of the B-58 bomber, the X-2 research plane, and several fighter planes, including the F-102 and F-105. Beginning in the 1950s, hypersonic tunnels were created to test flight at Mach 5 (five times the speed of sound). They required unusually high temperatures and speeds, and, because of power restrictions, runs had to be of short duration.

Since the 1960s, there have been several refinements in wind tunnels. Hypersonic tunnels can now operate much longer (one of them can provide continuous Mach 10 air flow). Helium has been used to create a Mach 50 blast of wind. Hydrogen and oxygen have been exploded to provide a blast wave of air. Electric explosions have been used to create shock waves. Wind tunnel technology now takes advantage of rapid advances in computerization, self-streamlining walls, **laser**-based instruments, cryogenic (freezing) operations, and magnetic model suspension.

*. Xenon

In the family of inert gases, xenon stands out as the only one that forms chemical compounds (mixtures) that are stable at room temperature. In 1962 British chemist Neil Bartlett created a stable compound of xenon, **platinum**, and **fluorine** ($XePtF_6$). This family of gases is often called *noble* rather than *inert*. Scientists soon formed compounds with some of xenon's sister elements, but none are stable under normal conditions. Although journalists at the time were quick to claim a revolution in chemistry, the possibility that noble gas compounds might exist had been predicted decades earlier, and their actual formation did little to revise scientific thought concerning chemistry.

Xenon gets its name from the Greek word for "strange" or "foreign" because it was so hard to find and understand. It was first isolated by Sir William Ramsay and British chemist Morris Travers in 1898. Earlier, Ramsay had discovered argon and **helium**. With Travers, he continued to search for the remaining elements in the inert gas family, which they theorized must exist due to the gases' position on the periodic table. They identified xenon by the characteristic color of its spectral lines. Xenon's atomic number is 54. The other members of the inert gas family are **neon**, **krypton**, and **radon**. Under ordinary conditions, xenon is a colorless, odorless, and tasteless gas that exists in the atmosphere in small quantities. Although traces are also found in minerals, air is the only commercial source of xenon, which is produced by separation from liquefied air.

Today, xenon is used in brilliant arc lamps for motion film projection,

Xenon gets its name from the Greek word for "strange" or "foreign" because it was so hard to find and understand.

in high-pressure ultraviolet radiation lamps, and in special flashbulbs used by photographers. One of xenon's radioactive **isotopes** (versions) is used to trace the movement of sands along the coasts of the ocean. Xenon has also found a niche in high-energy physics as a liquid used in bubble chambers, which detect nuclear radiation. Experimental applications of xenon include its use during diagnostic procedures to clarify **X-ray** pictures of the human brain.

X-ray

Few discoveries have been accompanied by as much fanfare as was that of the X-ray. During the 12 months following the publication of Wilhelm Röntgen's findings, more than 1,000 books and articles on the subject were written.

In 1895 while German physicist Wilhelm Röntgen was experimenting with a **cathode-ray tube,** he produced weak rays that caused a screen to fluoresce, or glow. In order to create a controlled environment, Röntgen placed the cathode tube in a black cardboard box, too thick for cathode rays to penetrate. Once the cathode-ray tube was turned on, however, Röntgen noticed that another screen across the room began to glow. Since this second screen was too far from the tube for cathode rays to reach, especially through a layer of cardboard, Röntgen realized that he had discovered a new type of ray.

Through experimentation Röntgen found that this new ray, unlike any others known at that time, was able to penetrate even the thick walls of his laboratory. Röntgen delivered a paper detailing his findings on December 28, 1895, in which he admitted that he did not know the precise nature of these new rays and chose to name them "X-rays," since "X" is the mathematical symbol for the unknown.

Few discoveries have been accompanied by as much fanfare as was that of the X-ray. During the 12 months following the publication of Röntgen's findings, more than 1,000 books and articles on the subject were written, and that number rose to more than 10,000 before 1910. The penetrating power of X-rays to reveal bone structure was immediately recognized by the medical community as a new diagnostic tool. However, not all of the excitement was positive, since many considered the X-ray machine's ability to look through walls and doors an end to personal privacy. In fact, opera houses banned the use of X-ray binoculars in order to prevent patrons from peering beneath the actresses' costumes. Nevertheless, more rational minds eventually prevailed, and Röntgen was awarded the first Nobel Prize for physics in 1901.

Practical Uses of X-rays

   X-rays are **electromagnetic waves**, like light waves, but with a wavelength about 1,000 times smaller. Because of this very short wavelength, X-rays can easily penetrate low-density material, such as flesh. However, they are still reflected or absorbed by high-density material, such as bone. The picture made by an X-ray machine shows the denser materials as dark areas. The first medical use of X-rays came in 1896 when the American

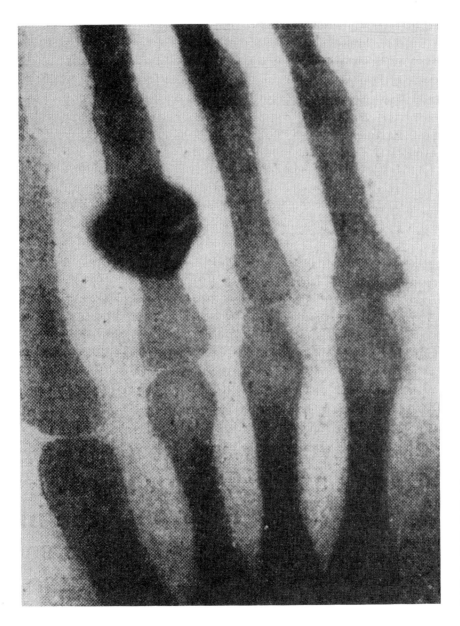

The first X-ray photograph, which was the right hand of Berth Röntgen, the wife of Wilhelm Röntgen, the discoverer of X-rays.

physiologist Walter Bradford Cannon used a fluorescent screen to follow the path of bismuth subnitrate through an animal's digestive system. Soon after, physicians worldwide began using X-rays on humans, usually to examine bone fractures or to search for foreign objects, such as bullets. Thomas Alva Edison invented the X-ray fluoroscope in 1896.

Tremendous advances in X-ray technology have been achieved since the turn of the century. One of the most exciting was the development of a new science, the field of X-ray crystallography. First conceived of by the German physicist Max von Laue, this science uses X-rays to probe the **molecular structure** of crystals.

X-ray crystallography has become an important tool for laboratory synthesis (creation) of many chemicals and drugs. **Penicillin**, which was in great demand during World War II (1939-45), was successfully synthesized by Dorothy Crowfoot Hodgkin. X-ray crystallography was also used to synthesize **insulin** and was instrumental in the discovery of the **DNA** (**deoxyribonucleic acid**) molecule.

One of the most familiar X-ray machines is the baggage scanner found at airport terminals. This low-power X-ray device is placed over a conveyor belt, where it scans passengers' luggage. The machine used in this type of scanner must operate at a very specific frequency—high enough to penetrate hard-shell baggage but low enough to prevent the accidental exposure of camera film.

The most important application of X-rays, however, remains their use in medicine. By 1970 most Americans were receiving at least one X-ray exam every year from physicians and dentists. However, recent evidence has shown that X-rays are potentially harmful and can lead to the development of leukemia. Many doctors thus recommend X-ray exams only when absolutely necessary. Ironically, the harmful side effects of X-rays have suggested yet another form of treatment, called radiotherapy. In this therapy, very high frequency X-rays ("hard rays") are used to destroy cancer cells. Radiotherapy is most often used in conjunction with chemotherapy (the treatment of disease by means of chemicals).

⋆⋆⋆ X-ray astronomy

X-ray astronomy is a product of the space age, and is one of the fastest-growing fields of astronomy. It involves not only X-ray stars, but galaxies, **pulsars**, **quasars**, and black holes as well.

X-rays were discovered quite by accident in 1895 by German physicist Wilhelm Röntgen. He noticed that barium crystals, which he had stored across the room, fluoresced (produced light) whenever he turned on a cathode-ray discharge tube. He correctly surmised that a previously unknown form of radiation of very short wavelengths, which he called X-rays, caused the crystals to glow.

Stars radiate energy in many other wavelengths than visible light, which is only one small part of the electromagnetic spectrum. At the low end are low-energy infrared radiation and radio wavelengths. Beyond the visible blue end of the spectrum are high-energy **ultraviolet radiation**, X-rays, and **gamma rays**.

There are two broad areas of X-ray astronomy. The first concerns soft X-rays located at the low end of the X-ray spectrum, overlapping longer ultraviolet wavelengths. The other concerns hard X-rays at the higher end of the electromagnetic spectrum, overlapping shorter gamma ray wavelengths.

The **ozone** layer of Earth's atmosphere shields the planet from high-energy radiation, preventing cosmic rays from reaching the surface. That is very fortunate, since such rays can be fatal to living organisms. Hard X-rays can be detected by instruments aboard balloons at high altitudes, as Victor Franz Hess discovered in 1911, but the only way to detect soft X-rays is to get above the atmosphere. American physicist Herbert Friedman accomplished this in the late 1940s. He used German V-2 rockets that had been captured during World War II (1939-45). Friedman placed X-ray detectors on board and launched them above the atmosphere. He was rewarded by discovering that the Sun emits X-rays.

X-ray Astronomy Takes Flight

Shortly after this discovery, a group of physicists from the Massachusetts Institute of Technology in Cambridge founded a company called American Science and Engineering, Inc. (ASEI). Its purpose was to study high-energy physics. When physicist Riccardo Giacconi joined the company in 1959, he and his colleagues concentrated on extraterrestrial X-ray sources and worked with National Aeronatics and Space Administration (NASA) to further Friedman's pioneering work.

Giacconi and ASEI devised a very sensitive X-ray telescope that could detect weak X-rays from specific areas of the sky. NASA placed this X-ray detector aboard an Arobee rocket for a six-minute flight on the night of June 18, 1962, that resulted in the first discovery of X-rays from inter-

X-ray astronomy really took off after an X-ray telescope discovered X-rays from interstellar space in 1962.

Interstellar Vocabulary

Binary star system: a system in which two stars circle around each other

Black hole: the remains of a large star that has collapsed, leaving behind a gravitational pull so strong that no light can escape

Galaxy: a group of star systems held together by gravity and separated from other such groups by large areas of space

NASA: the National Aeronautics and Space Administration, a government agency that plans and runs the U.S. space program

Neutron star: also called a **pulsar**

Pulsar: a dense spinning ball of interstellar matter

Stellar: an adjective from the Latin word for "star"

stellar space. (To be sure, there had been numerous equipment and rocket malfunctions before this success.) The detector had discovered emissions of X-rays coming from the constellation of Scorpius. Since this was the first source located in that constellation, it was named Scorpius X-1.

X-ray astronomy really "took off" after that. Additional X-ray sources were discovered in other parts of space on later flights. One was located at the Crab Nebula in Taurus, where a pulsar (neutron star) was later identified. Another was found in Cygnus (pronounced Sig-nus), called Cygnus X-1, where the X-rays are thought to be produced by a black hole in a **binary star** system.

The first X-ray galaxy, M87 (also known as Virgo A), was discovered in 1966. Astronomers believe most galaxies, including the Milky Way, emit weak X-rays. One galaxy, identified as NGC 5128 (also known as Centaurus A), is extremely strange, emitting ten times as much X-ray radiation as a normal galaxy. Other strong X-ray sources include the quasar 3C 273 and the Seyfert galaxy NGC 4151.

During the 1960s, Giacconi and Friedman actively urged NASA to build more complex X-ray satellites that could be placed in Earth's orbit. In December 1970 *Uhuru* was launched. It produced an extensive map of the X-ray sky. Later in the 1970s, three *High Energy Astronomical Observatories (HEAO)* were placed in orbit.

X-ray observations are very important in sorting out a wide variety of problems with great cosmological implications. X-rays offer clues about energy production deep in stellar interiors, the large-scale structure of the universe, and the strange properties of such compact exotic objects as pulsars and black holes.

See also **Electromagnetic wave**

X-ray machine

The very first X-ray device was discovered accidentally by the German scientist Wilhelm Röntgen in 1895. He found that a **cathode-ray tube** emitted certain invisible rays that could penetrate paper and wood, causing a screen of fluorescent material several yards away to glow. Though he used his device to examine the bone structure of the human hand, Röntgen's machine was really just a modified cathode-ray tube. True X-ray machines were not invented for several years.

Upon their discovery in 1895, X-rays were advertised as the new scientific wonder and were seized upon by entertainers. Circus patrons could view their own skeletons and were given pictures of their own bony hands wearing silhouetted jewelry. While many people were fascinated by this discovery, others feared that it would allow strangers to look through walls and doors and eliminate privacy.

What Are X-rays?

X-rays are waves of electromagnetic energy. They behave in much the same way as light rays, but at much shorter wavelengths (approximately 1,000 times shorter than light). When directed at a target, X-rays can often pass through the substance uninterrupted, especially when it is of low density. Higher density targets (such as the human body) will reflect or absorb the X-rays, because there is less space between the atoms for the short waves to pass through. Thus, an X-ray image shows dark areas where the rays traveled completely through the target (such as with flesh) and light areas where the rays were blocked by dense material (such as bone).

We are
probably most
familiar with
the type of
X-ray machine
used to examine
baggage at
airports.

X-ray Crystallography

At the same time the medical applications of X-rays were first explored, a new science was being founded. It was based on the principles introduced by German physicist Max von Laue (1879-1960). Laue theorized that crystals could be to X-rays what diffraction gratings were to visible light. He studied the interference pattern of X-rays passing through a crystal. These patterns revealed a great deal of information about the internal structure of the crystal. British physicists William Henry Bragg and his son William Lawrence Bragg took this field even further, developing a system of mathematics that could be used to interpret the interference patterns. This method became known as X-ray crystallography. It allowed scientists to study the structures of crystals with unsurpassed precision.

Crystallography has become an important tool for scientists, particularly those striving to synthesize chemicals (produce them artificially). By analyzing the information within a crystal's interference pattern, enough can be learned about that substance to create it artificially in a laboratory, and in large quantities. This technique was used to isolate the molecular structures of **penicillin**, **insulin**, and **DNA (deoxyribonucleic acid)**.

Medical Use of X-rays

Of course, the most important application of the X-ray has been its use in medicine. This importance was recognized almost immediately after Röntgen's findings were published in 1895. Within weeks of its first demonstration, an X-ray machine was used in America to diagnose bone fractures. Thomas Alva Edison invented an X-ray fluoroscope in 1896. American physiologist Walter Bradford Cannon used Edison's device to observe the movement of barium sulfate through the digestive system of animals and, eventually, humans. (Barium sulfate is a fine white powder that is still used as a contrast medium in X-ray photography of the digestive tract.) In 1913 the first X-ray tube designed specifically for medical purposes was developed by American chemist William Coolidge. X-rays have since become the most reliable method for diagnosing internal problems.

Modern medical X-ray machines have been grouped into two categories: those that generate "hard" X-rays and those that generate "soft"

X-rays. Soft X-rays are the kind used to photograph bones and internal organs; they operate at a relatively low frequency and, unless they are repeated too often, they cause little damage to **tissues**. Hard X-rays are very high frequency rays designed to destroy the molecules within specific cells, thus destroying tissue. Hard X-rays are used in radiotherapy, a treatment for cancer. Because of the high voltage necessary to generate hard X-rays, they are usually produced using cyclotrons or synchrotrons, which are variations of **particle accelerators** (atom smashers).

One of the more familiar X-ray machines is the security scanner used to examine baggage at airports. These machines use a very low-power scanner to illuminate the interior of purses and suitcases without causing damage to the contents, such as undeveloped film.

See also **Fluorescence and phosphorescence**

Wilhelm Röntgen accidentally discovered the very first X-ray device in 1895.

✦ Yeast

Yeasts are microscopic one-celled organisms that are classified in the kingdom *Fungi*. Since they lack chlorophyll, yeasts cannot make their own food as plants do. However, they have **cell** walls of cellulose and thus were formerly classified as plants.

The individual yeast cells multiply rapidly by the process of budding, in which a new cell begins as a small bulge along the cell wall of a parent cell. Soon huge populations of yeast cells gather, especially in the presence of an abundant food source. The cells often appear as long chains with newly formed cells still attached to their parent cells, due to the short budding time of just two hours.

Yeasts are among the few living things that do not need **oxygen** in order to produce energy. This oxygen-independent state is called anaerobic ("without oxygen"). During such anaerobic conditions, compounds produced by the yeast break down carbohydrates—starches and sugars—to form alcohol and **carbon dioxide** gas. This process is known as **fermentation** and it has been used for centuries in the production of certain foods and beverages.

Yeasts are among the few living things that do not need oxygen in order to produce energy.

Discovery of Yeast

Yeasts were first discovered by a French scientist, Charles Cagniard de Latour in 1857. He realized that these tiny structures were actually living cells that grow in number by budding and that cause fermentation. Further experiments on yeast fermentation were performed by French scientist Louis Pasteur, who showed that fermentation could take place only in the presence of living yeast cells. He also deduced that anaerobic conditions were necessary for proper fermentation of wine and beer. In the presence of oxygen, yeasts convert alcohol to **acetic acid**—vinegar.

The fermentation process of yeast is caused by enzymes, catalysts in chemical reactions similar to the digestive enzymes in the human body. (In fact the word **enzyme** means "in yeast.") Certain yeast enzymes act on starch to break down the long chain-like molecules into smaller units of sugar. Then other yeast enzymes convert one kind of sugar molecule to another. Still other enzyme reactions break apart the sugar molecule (composed of **carbon**, **hydrogen** and oxygen) into ethyl alcohol and carbon dioxide gas. The series of reactions provides the yeast cells with the energy necessary for their own growth and division.

The production of carbon dioxide and alcohol are merely by-products of processes necessary for the yeast to survive. But these by-products have

Wine-tasting contest in Paris, France, 1926. Yeast is traditionally added to liquids derived from grains and fruits to brew beer and wine. The natural starches and sugars provide food for the yeast and during fermentation the desired alcohol is released.

been used in human enterprise for centuries. Yeast is traditionally added to liquids derived from grains and fruits to brew beer and wine. The natural starches and sugars provide food for the yeast and during fermentation the desired alcohol is released.

Another variety of yeast is added to a dough made from the starchy portion of ground grains, such as wheat or rye flour. When this mixture is allowed to stand for a few hours, the yeast enzymes break down some of the starch and sugar, producing carbon dioxide. The carbon dioxide bubbles through the mixture, forming many air holes and causing the bread to rise. Since oxygen is present, no alcohol is produced when bread is rising. When the dough is baked, the air holes give the baked bread a lighter texture.

In the days before yeasts were made commercially, bread makers allowed yeasts from the air to furnish the enzymes necessary for the leavening (rising) of bread. Today two kinds of yeasts are available commercially, compressed and dry. Compressed yeast is made in small cakes that contain starch, yeast and enough moisture to start the fermentation process (and thus need refrigeration). Dry yeast is a powder mixture of yeast cells and corn meal that has been dried. It can be stored for long periods, giving it the advantage of a longer shelf life. Commercial yeast is made of ground grains mixed with filtered water. Sprouted grain or malt, which contains enzymes that convert starch to sugar, is added to the yeast mix, along with **bacteria**. The combination serves as food for live yeast cells. As the yeast ferments in the mixture, it is skimmed off, pressed, and made into yeast cakes.

In recent times, yeasts have been used to aid in the production of alternative energy sources. Yeasts are placed in huge vats of corn or other organic material. When fermentation takes place the yeasts convert the organic material into ethanol fuel. Geneticists are working on developing yeast strains that will convert even larger organic biomasses (living matter) into ethanol more efficiently.

Yellow fever

Yellow fever is an infectious disease affecting humans, monkeys, and several small mammals. It is caused by a **virus** and is carried by several species of mosquito. Yellow fever is found in Central and South American and in parts of Africa.

Yellow fever

This viral illness is characterized by the abrupt onset of headache, backache, rapidly rising fever, nausea, and vomiting. It usually attacks the liver, producing the jaundice (yellowing of the skin) which gives it its name. Yellow fever causes death in 2 to 5 percent of its cases. Those who survive it receive lifelong immunity. Other than reduction of the fever, no specific treatment is available for the sick person.

Yellow Fever Through History

Yellow fever was known on the coast of West Africa for centuries before the first epidemic occurred in the Western Hemisphere. That epidemic, reported in Barbados (West Indies) in 1647, probably resulted from the slave trade. The first epidemic in the United States occurred in New York City in 1668. By 1893, 135 major epidemics had occurred in North American port cities, with a death rate of 30 to 70 percent.

Yellow fever's scope of influence was wide. In 1802, 29,000 of the 33,000 soldiers sent by French emperor Napoleon to Santo Domingo (Dominican Republic) died in an epidemic. In 1881 construction on the Panama Canal by a company of French engineers was halted when more than 20,000 construction workers died of yellow fever and malaria (another infectious disease, also called "swamp fever").

Max Theiler received the Nobel Prize for physiology in 1951 for developing the first safe vaccine against yellow fever.

In the mid-1800s, yellow fever became a focus of scientific inquiry. In 1881 Cuban physician Carlos Juan Finlay correctly proposed the *Aëdes aegypti* species of mosquito as a carrier of yellow fever. In 1900 Walter Reed was appointed head of the U.S. Army Yellow Fever Board in Havana, Cuba. Working with Finlay, Reed's commission proved that *Aëdes aegypti* was indeed the carrier and that yellow fever was caused by an unknown microorganism.

Measures such as protecting infected patients from mosquito bites and eliminating mosquito breeding grounds were undertaken. By October 1901, no new cases of yellow fever were reported in Havana, Cuba. By 1906 no yellow fever remained in the Panama Canal Zone. Construction on the canal was completed in 1915. Mosquito eradication measures were tried in other areas where the disease was common, and the Western Hemisphere was almost free from yellow fever within a few years.

Vaccine Developed

In 1927 Reed's microorganism was found to be a virus. South African microbiologist Max Theiler and his assistant, Hugh Smith, working at Harvard University in Cambridge, Massachusetts, developed the first safe vaccine against yellow fever in 1936. It continues to be the only vaccine used by the World Health Organization in its ongoing efforts to immunize individuals living in areas where yellow fever occurs. Theiler received the Nobel Prize for physiology or medicine in 1951.

Because mosquito eradication is not possible in large, forested areas, yellow fever still occurs in parts of Central and South America and Africa. The most severe epidemic ever recorded occurred in Ethiopia (Africa) from 1960 to 1962, infecting 100,000 people and killing 30,000.

Besides the vaccine, the control of yellow fever depends upon the immunization of individuals entering a zone where the disease occurs, and the immunization of individuals leaving a zone where the disease occurs and entering one inhabited by *Aëdes aegypti* mosquitoes.

See also **Immune system**

⋆⋆ Yogurt

From early on in its history yogurt has been linked with long life and has even been used for medical purposes. No one is sure when yogurt was first developed, but some scholars think it was in Biblical times. Legend has it that the patriarch Abraham offered yogurt to the angels when they told him of the birth of his son Isaac. Over the years, yogurt has been credited with Abraham's long life. He is said to have lived to the advanced age of 175. Some Biblical scholars believe that yogurt is the milk referred to in the Biblical phrase that describes Israel as "the land of milk and honey."

In the early 1500s, a Turkish doctor prescribed a diet of yogurt for King François I (1494-1547). The treatment was credited with saving the life of the French monarch. From that point on, yogurt was dubbed *le lait de la vie eternelle,* or "the milk of eternal life," by the French.

In the early 1900s, a group of Bulgarian peasants were said to be extremely healthy and to be bearing children past the age of 100. The story

Some Biblical scholars believe that yogurt is the milk referred to in the Biblical phrase that describes Israel as "the land of milk and honey."

attracted the attention of Elie Metchnikoff (1845-1916), a Russian bacteriologist (a scientist who studies bacteria). When he went to observe the aged Bulgarian farmers, Metchnikoff found that yogurt played a large role in their diet. The peasants would frequently pause from their work and eat large bowls of yogurt mixed with onions, nuts, and vegetables. Metchnikoff became convinced that yogurt was responsible for their incredible strength and long life. He began to study the food. In time he isolated (separated out) two strains of bacteria that were present in yogurt: *Streptococcus thermophilus* and *lactobacillus bulgaricus* (named for the country in which Metchnikoff discovered it). Metchnikoff discovered that these bacteria are rich in B **vitamins,** which combat a common intestinal virus. Metchnikoff believed this virus produced toxins (poisons) that speed the aging process. In addition to killing this intestinal virus, yogurt is easily digested and aids in the digestion of other foods. Good digestion is a key to staying healthy.

Yogurt Comes to America

In 1929 Isaac Carasso, a Frenchman who lived in Paris, began selling yogurt commercially. He named his product "Danone," or "little Daniel" after his son. In 1942, Daniel came to the United States with his father's recipe, and introduced the product as Dannon. By the 1950s, Carasso had the largest yogurt-producing factory in the world. By the mid-1960s, yogurt had established itself in America's fast-growing "health food" market.

Yogurt is no longer a special product found only in health food stores. Yogurt, in many flavors and sizes, can now be found in most supermarket dairy cases. The food is even packaged in single serving containers, and commercials advertise it to students and weight watchers. In the 1980s, frozen yogurt stores, offering a healthy alternative to ice cream, were among the fastest-growing franchises in America.

⋆ Zero

Zero is a unique number, belonging to neither the positive or negative number set. Although zero is first in number order, it was the very last number symbol to be discovered. Among the ancient Babylonian civilizations of 600 B.C. and earlier, a space was only sometimes used to indicate an "empty place." Despite its potential for confusion, the method appears to have been acceptable for several centuries. It was not until the introduction of counting boards, the abacus, and place value notations that the empty space began to be filled with a symbol.

The first zero symbol was believed to have originated in the fourth century B.C. by an unknown Indian mathematician. When he wanted to record a more permanent answer on his beaded counting board, he used a simple dot. This was called a *sunya* and indicated columns in which there were no beads. While the sunya was not the true zero symbol that is used today, its use in place value notation was very important.

By A.D. 600, Brahmi Mahavira began using zero as a number in calculations, unlike earlier mathematicians who had used the zero symbol only to denote the absence of a number. About the year 900, Arab mathematicians introduced what is today known as the Hindu-Arabic numeral system. The zero symbol was indicated by a dot, or *sifr,* as it was called in Arabic. Sifr became "cipher" when adopted into English, and also it took on the meaning "to calculate." The dot gradually evolved to a small circle and it eventually became the familiar oval we recognize today.

The zero symbol reached Europe about the twelfth century. However, it was not eagerly received. Reluctant to abandon their familiar Roman numerals, many Europeans revolted against the new Hindu-Arabic symbols. A hostile battle ensued between the partisans of the two systems that sometimes resulted in bloodshed. By 1500, almost 400 years after its introduction in Europe, the Hindu-Arabic numbers were accepted and adopted as our standard numerals.

⋆⋆ Zipper

The zipper was invented by mechanical engineer Whitcomb L. Judson, who was tired of having to fasten his fashionable high-buttoned boots.

The zipper was invented by Whitcomb L. Judson, a Chicago, Illinois, mechanical engineer. Tired of having to fasten his fashionable high-buttoned boots by hand, Judson invented the Clasp Locker and patented it in 1893. It consisted of a movable guide that meshed together two sets of hooks and eyes. Judson also invented the machine that could mass produce his fasteners. However, the machine broke down frequently and the fastener itself had a way of coming undone unexpectedly.

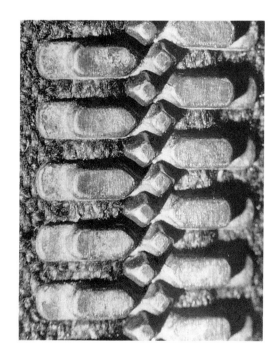

New and Improved

In 1905 Judson invented an improved fastener, the C-curity. Like its predecessor, it tended to break open. Perhaps for this reason, clothing manufacturers showed no interest in the device.

It was Gideon Sundback, a Swedish engineer employed by Judson, who developed the first really practical and successful slide fastener. Sundback's 1913 invention used small, interlocking teeth that were flexible and remained locked together. Sundback also invented efficient machinery to produce his improved fastener cheaply. (Meanwhile, over in Europe, Catharina Kuhn-Moos patented a similar fastener the same year.)

Although the slide fastener was now ready to be mass-produced, clothing manufacturers continued to ignore it—except for one, a company that agreed in 1918 to supply the U.S. Navy with flying suits equipped with the device. Judson's company suddenly had an order for thousands of the fasteners.

Manufacturers began to realize how useful the fastener could be. Soon it appeared on gloves and tobacco pouches. In 1923 the B. F. Goodrich Company added the slide fasteners to their **rubber** galoshes. Their new footwear design was called "Zippers." From then on, "zipper" became the popular name for the fastener itself. Zippers next appeared on clothing, first in men's pants, and, in the late 1920s, in women's garments. Today's design is little changed from Sundback's original.

See also **Buttons and other fasteners**

Master Index

A

Abacists *5:* 904
Abacus *2:* 298; *5:* 904
Abbe, Cleveland *6:* 1067, 1148
Abdomen *4:* 662
Abelson, Philip *4:* 730
Abercromby, Ralph *6:* 1149
Abortion *5:* 907
Abplanalp, Robert H. *1:* 19
Abrasive *1:* **1-2**
Absolute scale *1:* 3
Absolute zero *1:* **2-3**
Acetaminophen *3:* 571
Acetic acid *1:* **3-4,** 7; *5:* 845; *6:* 1170
Acetylcholine *1:* **4-6**; *6:* 1040
Acheson, Edward G. *1:* 1
Acid *1:* 3, 9; *4:* 740
Acid and base *1:* 4, **6-9**; *3:* 563
Acid rain *1:* **9-12**; *4:* 744
Acoustics, physiological *1:* **12-13**
Acquired blindness *2:* 409
Acromegaly *3:* 560
Acropolis *1:* 11
Acrylic plastic *1:* 13-14
Acrylonitrile *3:* 459
ACTH (adrenocorticotropic hormone) *1:* **14-15**; *3:* 553
Actinium *5:* 820
Acupuncture *1:* **15-17**
Adams, John Couch *4:* 728; *5:* 845

Adams' New York Gum *2:* 265
Adams, Thomas, Jr. *2:* 265
Adams, Thomas, Sr. *2:* 265
Addison's disease *3:* 553
Addison, Thomas *3:* 553
Addition *1:* 38; *2:* 227, 274, 281, 294, 299
Additive three-color process *2:* 278
Ader, Clement *6:* 1019
Adhesives and adhesive tape *1:* **17-19**; *2:* 345; *5:* 853, 856
Adiabatic demagnetization *2:* 331
Adipose tissue *3:* 447
Adrenal gland cortex hormones *3:* 552
Adrenalin *1:* 5
Advanced X-ray Astrophysics Facility (AXAF) *6:* 1005
Advertising *3:* 550
Advil *3:* 572
Aëdes aegypti *6:* 1172
Aero Foam *3:* 462
Aerodynamics *6:* 1157
Aeronautics *6:* 1157
Aerosol spray *1:* 19-20
Agate *3:* 444
Agent Orange *2:* 263
Agricultural crops *2:* 336
Agriculture *3:* 453, 499, 500
AIDS (Acquired Immune Deficiency Syndrome) *1:*

20-24; *2:* 246, 263; *3:* 497, 541, 575; *5:* 848, 893; *6:* 1134
AIDS therapies and vaccines *1:* **24-26**
Aiken, Howard *2:* 300
Air *2:* 241
Airbag, automobile *1:* **26-27**
Air conditioning *1:* **27-29**
Aircraft *1:* 14, 19, **29-36,** 41, 46; *2:* 305; *3:* 459, 585, 594, 535; *4:* 635, 688, 703; *5:* 925, 933, 927; *6:* 1014, 1019, 1035, 1156
Airplane *4:* 761; *6:* 1000
Air pollution *1:* 9; *3:* 514; *4:* 774; *5:* 824
Airship *3:* 564
Airy, George Biddle *2:* 411
alaia *6:* 1036
Alchemy *3:* 562; *6:* 1088
Alcohol *2:* 245; *3:* 450, 509; *6:* 1170, 1171
Alcohol, distilling of *1:* **37-38**
Alcoholic hepatitis *3:* 542
Alcoholism *1:* 37
Aldrin, Edwin "Buzz" *4:* 710; *6:* 984
Aleksandrov, Pavel Sergeevich *6:* 1076
Alexanderson, Ernst *6:* 1058
Algebra *5:* 884
Algorists *5:* 905
Algorithm *1:* **38**; *2:* 227
Alhazen *4:* 653

Boldfaced numbers indicate main entry pages; italicized numbers indicate volume number

Boldfaced numbers indicate main entry pages; italicized numbers indicate volume number

Boldfaced numbers indicate main entry pages; italicized numbers indicate volume number

Comic strip and comic book
2: 284-286; 5: 927
Communication 2: 310, 315,
348; 3: 449, 456; 4: 639
Communications satellite 2:
227, 286-289; 4: 704; 6:
1055
Compact disc player 2: 289-
290; 4: 699
Compact discs 6: 1019, 1141
Compass 2: 290-292, 371,
386; 4: 725
Compound 2: 238, 241; 3: 593
Compressed air illness 2: 339
Compressed yeast 6: 1171
Compression and transfer
molding 5: 854
Compression wave 6: 1107
Comptometer 2: 229
Compton, Arthur Holly 4: 655
Computer 1: 38; 2: 293, 331,
348, 384; 3: 551; 4: 644,
695; 5: 900
Computer, analog 2: 293-294,
302; 4: 697
Computer application 2: 294-
297, 307
Computer art 2: 317
Computer-Assisted Instruction
(CAI) 6: 1047
Computer chip 5: 869
Computer, digital 2: 227, 254,
292, 298-302, 305, 308,
312, 316, 333, 406; 3: 450;
4: 665, 697; 5: 880, 900;
6: 1079, 1130
Computer disk and tape 2:
303-305, 310; 4: 697; 5:
836
Computer graphics 2: 348
Computer, industrial uses of
2: 305-307, 312, 316, 333,
348; 5: 900
Computer input and output
device 2: 307, 308-310,
311, 312, 316, 348; 4: 666,
697; 5: 933; 6: 1130, 1139
Computer Integrated
Manufacturing 2: 307
Computer network 2: 310-
311, 312; 4: 697
Computer operating system 2:
305, 311-312, 333; 4: 666;
6: 1035

Computer output microfilm 2:
310
Computer scientist 2: 302
Computer simulation 2: 307,
313-315
Computer speech recognition
2: 310, 315-316, 348; 6:
1130
Computer storage 3: 551
Computer technology 2: 405
Computer vision 2: 307, 310,
316-317
Concave lenses 4: 648
Concentrated fruit juice 2:
317-318
Concord Academy 6: 1045
Concorde 1: 36; 3: 596
Concrete and cement 2: 368;
6: 1084
Condensed milk 2: 236
Condenser 1: 37
Conditioned reflex 5: 814
Conduction 3: 532
Congenital blindness 2: 409
Conjunctivitis 2: 409
Contact lens 2: 318-319, 412
Containers 2: 401
Contaminant 2: 336
Continental drift 2: 319-322,
370; 4: 758; 5: 843, 844,
880; 6: 1117
Contraception 5: 908
Convection 3: 532
Convex lenses 4: 648
Conveyor belt 2: 349; 5: 829
Cookie 2: 266
Coolidge, William 6: 1166
Cooper, Leon 6: 1035
Cooper, Peter 6: 1081
Copernicus, Nicolaus 3: 482,
484; 5: 838, 943; 6: 1032
Copper 2: 384; 3: 538, 591;
4: 758; 6: 1068, 1088
Coral Draw 2: 297
Corliss, George 6: 1018
Cornea 2: 318
Corneal contact lenses 2: 318
Corneal sculpting 5: 872
Corning Glass Works 3: 456
Corning, Leonard 2: 278
Corona 6: 1033
Coronagraph 5: 947
Coronagraphic photometer 5:
947

Corpuscular theory 4: 654
Corrosive 1: 3
Cortisone 2: 322, 269; 3: 552;
4: 657
Cosmetics 2: 322-326; 3:
519, 520; 4: 764
Cosmic ray 3: 488; 5: 866,
948; 6: 1022, 1111, 1125,
1163
Cosmological principle 6:
1012
Cosmos 5: 912
Cosmos and Damian 6: 1090
Cowcatcher 6: 1081
Cowen, Joshua 3: 467
Cowpox 3: 576
Crab nebula 3: 488
Crack 2: 278
Cramer, Stuart W. 1: 28
Crane 2: 249; 5: 897
Crapper, Thomas 6: 1073
Cray, Seymour 6: 1034
Creed, Frederick G. 6: 1051
Crest 6: 1075
Cretaceous catastrophe 2:
326-329
Crick, Francis 2: 354, 404; 3:
547
Crime 2: 277; 3: 460, 501
Crime prevention 4: 649, 657
Criminal 4: 649
Cro-Magnon man 3: 558
Crookes, William 4: 743; 6:
1064
Crops 2: 336
Cross, Charles Frederick 5:
842
Cruise control, automobile 2:
329-330
Cryogenics 2: 330-331; 3: 538
Cryolite 3: 470
Cryopreservation 3: 588
Cryosurgery 2: 255
Crystal 5: 877; 6: 1162
Crystallography 2: 355; 6:
1162
Crystal rectifiers 4: 646
Cummings, Alexander 6:
1073
Cure 2: 331
Curie, Marie 2: 331; 5: 877,
881
Curie, Pierre 2: 331; 5: 837,
877, 881

Boldfaced numbers indicate main entry pages; italicized numbers indicate volume number

G

Boldfaced numbers indicate main entry pages; italicized numbers indicate volume number

H

Haber, Fritz *3:* 456; *4:* 743
Hafnium *2:* 390; *5:* 820
Haggerty, Patrick *2:* 228
Hair care *3:* **519-521**
Hair-care products *2:* 326
Hair dryer *3:* 519
Hair dyes *3:* 520
Hair extensions *3:* 520
Hairpiece *3:* 520
Hair spray *3:* 520
Hair weaving *3:* 521
Haldane, John Burdon *2:* 404;
    4: 722; *5:* 855
Hale, George Ellery *5:* 946;
    6: 1055
Hall, Chester Moor *6:* 1054
Halley, Edmond *4:* 690, 738;
    6: 1148
Hall, Lloyd A. *3:* 476
Hall, Samuel Read *6:* 1045
Hallucinogen *3:* **521-523**
Halogen lamp *2:* 394; *3:* **523-
    524**
Halol *6:* 1088
Haloperidol *6:* 1088
Halsted, William *2:* 277
Haltran *3:* 572
Hamilton, Alice *4:* 741
Hammond, Laurens *4:* 720
Hancock, Thomas *5:* 905
Handguns *2:* 273
Hanway, Jonas *6:* 1115
Hard disk *2:* 303
Hard drive *2:* 305
Harder, Delmar S. *2:* 333
Harding, Warren G. *5:* 875
Hardy, Godfrey Harold *5:* 855
Hardy-Weinberg equilibrium
    5: 855
Harington, Sir John *6:* 1072
Harmine *3:* 522
Harpoon *3:* **524-525**
Harrington, George F. *2:* 340
Harrington, Joseph *2:* 307
Harris, Geoffrey *3:* 553
Harris, John *6:* 1074
Harrison, Michael *5:* 860
Harrison, Ross Granville *4:*
    734
Harris, Rollin *2:* 293
Hartley, Walter Noel *4:* 772
Hart, William Aaron *4:* 723

Harvard Graphics *2:* 297
Hashish *3:* 522
Hata, Sahachiro *6:* 1043
Hausdorff, Felix *6:* 1076
Hawking radiation *3:* 527
Hawking, Stephen William *3:*
    526-527
Healing *1:* 15
Health *2:* 256, 263, 269, 339,
    343; *3:* 447, 468, 471, 478,
    504; *4:* 673, 682, 687; *5:*
    805
Hearing *1:* 12
Hearing aids and implants *3:*
    528-529; *4:* 697
Hearing impairment *2:* 315;
    5: 921
Heart *2:* 256
Heart defects, congenital *3:*
    530
Heart disease *2:* 269, 382
Heart-lung machine *3:* **529-
    530**
Heat *1:* 27; *2:* 385; *3:* 526; *4:*
    688
Heat and thermodynamics *1:*
    3; *3:* **530-532**; *5:* 924
Heating *3:* **532-535**
Heat pump *3:* 535
Heat-resistant glass *6:* 1055
Heezen, Bruce Charles *4:* 704
Heezen-Ewing theory *4:* 704
Heinlein, Robert A. *6:* 1143
Heisenberg, Werner *5:* 865,
    866, 889
Helicopter *1:* 33, 36; *3:* 503,
    535-537; *6:* 1078
Heliocentric theory *5:* 838
Heliography *5:* 832
Helium *2:* 330; *3:* **537-539**,
    599; *4:* 637, 726; *5:* 866,
    883; *6:* 1033, 1159
Helmont, Jan Baptista van *3:*
    569
Hemley, R. J. *3:* 566
Hemophilia *3:* 497, 539-541;
    5: 920
Hench, Philip *1:* 14; *3:* 552
Henie, Sonja *3:* 573
Henry, Edward R. *3:* 461
Henry, Prince of Portugal *2:*
    291
Hepatitis *1:* 15; *3:* **541-542,**
    584

Heredity *2:* 269, 333, 404; *3:*
    493, 498, 499, 522, 539,
    543-547; *4:* 688
Heroin *3:* 547; *4:* 713
Hero of Alexandria *4:* 653; *5:*
    900
Herpes *2:* 263; *3:* 542, 584
Herschel, William *3:* 461; *4:*
    677, 728; *5:* 913; *6:* 1054,
    1118, 1119
Hershey Chocolate Company
    2: 267
Hershey, Milton S. *2:* 267
Hertz *1:* 45; *2:* 385
Hertz, Heinrich Rudolph *2:*
    388; *3:* 590; *4:* 655; *5:* 829
Hess, Harry Hammond *2:*
    321; *4:* 705
Hess, Victor Franz *6:* 1163
Hevelius, Johann *4:* 710
Hevesy, György *3:* 594
Hewish, Antony *5:* 863
Hieroglyphics *1:* 41
Higgs particle *5:* 810
High-definition television
    (HDTV) *2:* 227; *3:* 459; *6:*
    1060
*High Energy Astrophysical
    Observatories* (HEAO) *3:*
    488; *6:* 1005
High-pressure physics *3:* **547-
    548**
High risk behavior *1:* 20
High-speed flash photography
    3: **548-549**
Highways *2:* 329
Hildebrand, Alan *2:* 329
Hilyer, Andrew Franklin *3:*
    535
Hindenburg *1:* 33
Hindu-Arabic numerals *5:*
    905
Hinton, William A. *6:* 1043
Hippocrates *4:* 717
Histamine *1:* 39
Histology *6:* 1069, 1070
Hitchings, George *2:* 263
Hitler, Adolf *1:* 6
H.L. *Hunley* *6:* 1078
H.M.S. *Challenger* *4:* 757
Hockey *3:* 572
Hodge, P. R. *3:* 464
Hodgkin, Dorothy Crowfoot
    5: 817; *6:* 1162

Boldfaced numbers indicate main entry pages; italicized numbers indicate volume number

Boldfaced numbers indicate main entry pages; italicized numbers indicate volume number

Lucy *3:* 559

Lumière, Auguste *2:* 279; *4:* 715, 716

Lumière, Louis *2:* 279; *4:* 715, 716

Luna 1 *6:* 994

Luna 2 *4:* 711

Luna 3 *4:* 711; *6:* 994

Luna 9 *6:* 994

Lunar eclipses *4:* 709

Lunar topography *4:* 710

Lung cancer *3:* 497

Lungs *3:* 529

Lunokhod 1 *4:* 712

Luvs *2:* 345

Lyell, Charles *2:* 403; *6:* 1117

Lyme disease *4:* **661**

Lymphatic system *4:* **662-663**

Lymph glands *4:* 662

Lymphocytes *4:* 662

Lyot, Bernard *5:* 947

M

McAdam, John *5:* 895

McCollum, Elmer V. *6:* 1137

McCormick, Cyrus *4:* 680

Machine language *4:* **665-666**

Machine tools *4:* 679

Machine vision *2:* 317

Macintosh, Charles *6:* 1143

McKay, Frederick S. *3:* 468

McMillan, Edwin *4:* 730

Machine gun *1:* 31

Magellan *6:* 997, 1129

Magic Tape *1:* 19

MAGLEV technology *6:* 1084

Magnesium *1:* 10; *4:* **667-668,** 712

Magnet *2:* 382; *5:* 809

Magnetic core memory *4:* 672

Magnetic declination *2:* 291, 370

Magnetic dip *2:* 370, 387

Magnetic field *2:* 331; *3:* 487, 599; *4:* **668,** 752; *5:* 921, 948; *6:* 1035, 1108, 1128

Magnetic levitation *6:* 1084

Magnetic recording *2:* 303; *4:* **668-670,** 697, 699, 745; *6:* 1019, 1132

Magnetic resonance *4:* 753

Magnetic resonance imaging (MRI) *4:* **670-671,** 753

Magnetic tape *2:* 308; *4:* 668

Magnetism *2:* 291, 385, 387

Magnetometer *4:* 757

Magneto-optical shutter *3:* 548

Magnetophon *4:* 669

Magnifying glass *6:* 1038

Magnitude *2:* 366

Mahoney, John F. *6:* 1044

Maiman, Theodore Harold *2:* 290; *3:* 551; *4:* 641

Mainframe *2:* 298

Mainframe computer *2:* 295, 310, 312; *4:* **671-673,** 705

Makeup *2:* 322

Malaise *3:* 541

Malaria *2:* 336; *6:* 1172

Malleus *1:* 13

Malpighi, Marcello *4:* 662

Mammals *2:* 326

Mammography *4:* **673-674**

Manby, George William *3:* 462, 464

Manganese *4:* **674-676**; *6:* 1048

Manhattan Project *2:* 376; *3:* 567; *4:* 748, 753

Mannes, Leopold *2:* 279

Manufacturing *2:* 282, 305, 317; *3:* 562

Manuscripts *2:* 400

Mao, H. K. *3:* 566

Map *2:* 291; *3:* 449

Marcel waves *3:* 519

Marconi, Guglielmo *3:* 590; *4:* 635; *5:* 875, 920; *6:* 1056

Marey, Etienne-Jules *4:* 716

Margarine *3:* 448

Maria *4:* 710

Marie-Davy, Edme Hippolyte *6:* 1148

Marijuana *3:* 522

Mariner 2 *5:* 948; *6:* 1128

Mariner 9 *5:* 912

Mariner 10 *4:* 687; *5:* 942

Mark I *2:* 300, 302

Mars *2:* 242; *4:* **676-678,** 729; *5:* 911, 912, 945; *6:* 995, 1118

Marum, Martin van *4:* 772

Maser *4:* 702, 765

Mash *1:* 37

Masking tape *1:* 18

Mason, Walter *2:* 342

Mass production *2:* 252, 326, 333, 394; *4:* **678-681**

Mass spectrograph *4:* **681-682**

Mass spectrometer *4:* 681

Mass transit *6:* 1028

Math *1:* 38; *2:* 228, 293; *3:* 483, 485, 593; *5:* 855, 883; *6:* 1075

Mathematical modeling *6:* 1147

Mathijsen, Antonius *3:* 478

Matrix mechanics *5:* 865

Matrix theory *5:* 868

Matsushita *6:* 1132

Matter *3:* 512

Mauchly, John *2:* 303

Maxim, Hiram *3:* 519

Maxim silencer *3:* 517

Maxwell, James Clerk *2:* 388; *4:* 655; *5:* 867

Maya *2:* 264, 266

Maybach, Wilhelm *3:* 586

Mayer, Tobias *4:* 710

Maytag Company *6:* 1142

Mazzitello, Joe *6:* 1131

Me 262 *3:* 595

Measles *3:* 542, 575; *6:* 1134

Medawar, Peter *3:* 575; *6:* 1092

Medical diagnostic devices *4:* 674

Medical technology *2:* 254, 256, 263, 343, 382, 383, 393, 405; *3:* 456, 468, 478, 495, 497, 499, 528, 529, 575, 581, 583, 587; *4:* 640, 670, 674, 713, 747, 751; *5:* 805, 806, 809, 849, 859, 872, 881, 891, 908; *6:* 1030, 1041, 1090, 1108, 1151

Medicine *2:* 322, 343; *3:* 478, 549, 571, 583; *4:* 640

Medipren *3:* 572

Meiosis *3:* 494

Melanoma *3:* 496

Melin, Spud *3:* 480

Mendel, Gregor *2:* 271, 352, 404; *3:* 495, 545

Mendeleev, Dmitry I. *5:* 820, 821

Boldfaced numbers indicate main entry pages; italicized numbers indicate volume number

Boldfaced numbers indicate main entry pages; italicized numbers indicate volume number

Boldfaced numbers indicate main entry pages; italicized numbers indicate volume number

Boldfaced numbers indicate main entry pages; italicized numbers indicate volume number

Boldfaced numbers indicate main entry pages; italicized numbers indicate volume number

Boldfaced numbers indicate main entry pages; italicized numbers indicate volume number

Boldfaced numbers indicate main entry pages; italicized numbers indicate volume number